The MeeTwo Teenage Mental Help Handbook

We'd like to say a huge thank you to all the amazing young people from across the UK who are currently using the MeeTwo app. Listening to you and learning more about what you need has been the inspiration for this handbook Without you, none of this would have been possible.

Sales & Marketing
Sharmaine Malik

Youth Engagement and Fundraising
Kerstyn Comley
Thomas Freeney

Press
Hilly Janes

Schools and Universities
Mulberry UTC, Tower Hamlets
Churston Ferrers Grammar School, Devon
London College of Communication,
University of the Arts London
Park High School, Middlesex
Sylvia Young Theatre School, London

Sponsors
The Texel Foundation
Teach First
Santander
EXPO Live

Supporters
Mermaids
Kooth
Humane Engineering
Gendered Intelligence
Family Planning Association
Ipnos Software Inc
Neybox Digital Ltd
Osborne Cawkwell
Educational Consultants
Flo Health Inc
The Sleep Council

Published by MeeTwo Education Ltd
Printed in the United Kingdom by Park Communications
First Printing, 2018

ISBN 978-1-9164959-9-9

Editor & Creative Director
Suzi Godson
Assistant
Scarlet Evans

Photography
Freddie Marriage
Katy English
Scarlet Evans
Ellen Pearson
Alexander Kireev
Eugenia Maximo
Suzi Godson
Stroma Cairns
Bebeplace
Creative Commons
Unsplash
Pixabay

Illustrations
Yumi Sakagawa
Katie Lennard
Katie Jordan
Josie Chiswell Jones
Dinah Hall
Ruby Evans
Amber Evans
Velvet Lowe

Yumi Sakagawa illustrations are excerpted from her beautiful books 'Your Illustrated Guide to Becoming One With the Universe' and 'There is No Right Way to Meditate' Copyright © 2014 & 2015 by Yumi Sakugawa and published by Adams Media, a division of Simon and Schuster, Inc. Used with permission of the publisher. All rights reserved.

Transcription
Isobel Hewitt

Proofreading
Rachel Carlyle

Interns
Lydia Torrington
Urvi & Adrea

Supreme Patience
Tim Lowe
Ian Comley

We've done our best, but if you do find a typo in this publication, do us a huge favour and email us at info@meetwo.co.uk

The 'epidemic of teenage depression and anxiety' sweeping across the UK is front page news, but in all the media noise, one voice has been conspicuously absent. Yours.

Not any more. The MeeTwo Teenage Mental Help Handbook lets you tell your stories, in your words. And because we know you need help, not headlines, we've created an ace directory packed with cool, clever, creative ways to help you to help yourself. If you turn the book around you'll find awesome interviews with leading experts in teenage mental health too.

The MeeTwo Teenage Mental Help Handbook is not a school book. You won't be tested on any of it. You don't even have to read it. But we think you might want to.

About the MeeTwo app. Everyone knows that when you feel down, talking to someone who cares really helps. But you might not realise that when you are having a hard time, one of the most effective ways to make yourself happier is to share those feelings with someone else who is having the same problem.

That's how the MeeTwo app works. By sharing both your worries and your solutions, everyone ends up getting the support they need. Often, just realising that you are not the only one, or that what you are going through is actually kind of normal, is enough to make you feel less anxious.

MeeTwo is safe because every post and reply gets screened before it goes live. And it's anonymous, so you can talk about virtually anything. It's quick and easy to use. Oh, and it's free. Why not give it a try?

The MeeTwo app

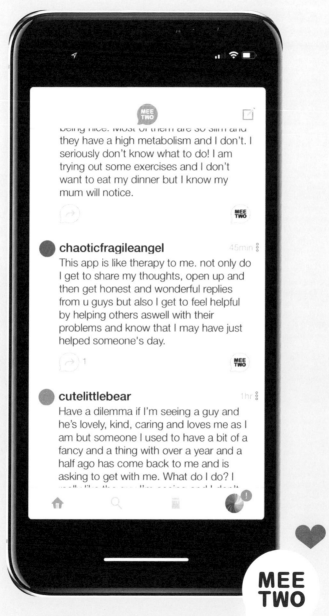

being nice. Most of them are so slim and they have a high metabolism and I don't. I seriously don't know what to do! I am trying out some exercises and I don't want to eat my dinner but I know my mum will notice.

chaoticfragileangel   45min

This app is like therapy to me. not only do I get to share my thoughts, open up and then get honest and wonderful replies from u guys but also I get to feel helpful by helping others aswell with their problems and know that I may have just helped someone's day.

1

cutelittlebear   1hr

Have a dilemma if I'm seeing a guy and he's lovely, kind, caring and loves me as I am but someone I used to have a bit of a fancy and a thing with over a year and a half ago has come back to me and is asking to get with me. What do I do? I

99 PROBLEMS. ONE SOLUTION

MEE TWO

The first print run of The MeeTwo Mental Help Handbook was funded by a Kickstarter campaign. Without the support of everyone on this list, it would never have been published. Their generosity means that young people across the country now have access to this unique resource.

Karen Hanton
Nigel Bliss
Don & Julie Godson
Adrian Court
Ian Nairn
Isamaya Ffrench
Kim Morrish
Liberty Global Group
Pat Wheeler Jones
Simon Tuttle

Æthan Ffrench
Alex
Athena Paginton
Bea McIntosh
Becky Schutt
Ben Clarke
Benedicte Gercke
Bridget Connell
Caroline Morton
Caroline Wagstaff
Cathy Taylor
Celia Briggs
Chris Dyson
Chris Mott
Clare Singleton
Clement Camilleri
David Wilkinson
Dorian McFarland
Elizabeth
Elizabeth Cooper
Elizabeth Wilson
Erica Wolfe-Murray
F Kramer
Fiona Colquhoun
Fran Needham
Frances Torrington
Inaki Izcue
J Chevallier
Janita Tan
Jayne Simpson
Jemma Lawley
Jenni Newcombe
Jennifer Singer
Jenny Baggs

Jessica Dimbleby
Jonathan Pryce
Jill Reidy
Josine Sahakian
Ju Yen Tan
Jules Pancholi
Julie Weeds
K Riegler
Kathryn
Kathy Coach
Laura Mills
Laura Ronchini
Lauren Wilson
Lesley Annand
Lidka Semetilo
Michael Gorgy
Michael Norton
Michael Wilson
Mike Jenkinson
Moritz Platt
Neil Johnson
Nibs Webber
Nicholas Hillen
NIPS
Omer Moghraby
Paul Summerfield
Ross Taylor
Ruby Evans
Sandy Foskett
Sophie Brandon
Sophie Lidbetter
Starmaru
Stef and Alice Mastropietro
Susie Atkinson
Susie Schutt
The Creative Fund
Thomas Freeney
Tim Ryder
Tim Spence
Tosh Kojima
Tracey Essery
Verena Hewat
Verity Bramwell
Zoe Berger

PERSONAL STORIES

THE MENTAL HELP DIRECTORY

This directory has been designed to give you the tools to help yourself, no matter what the problem is. Each double page spread lists useful and effective support groups, helplines, apps, books, self-help and media, as well as fun activities that can help you to feel better.

EXPERT ANALYSIS

ANXIETY IS A HEAVY ROCK...
BY YUMI SAKUGAWA

YELLING AT IT WON'T MAKE IT GO AWAY...

I HATE YOU FOR BEING SO HEAVY AND HARD

BUT SOMETIMES, IF YOU TAKE THE TIME TO FEEL THE TEXTURE AND RIDGES OF YOUR ANXIETY.....

IT FEELS JUST A LITTLE LESS HEAVIER THAN IT WAS BEFORE.

We ♥ Yumi Sakugawa

Toby is a talented young poet and spoken word performer.
He wrote this poem for MeeTwo and we made it into a film
with the help of students at the Sylvia Young Theatre School.
You can see it on our website at www.meetwo.co.uk

MEE
TWO

Thanks Toby!

I am so lonesome and glum
Punched a wall today
I think I might have broken my thumb
Oh to be young

Sometimes I can't breathe I feel so much panic
My grades are going down like the boat Titanic
If I don't scrape a C in this exam I am dead
Oh to be a teen and to have it all ahead

I'm in love with my best friend's boyfriend
it's totally brutal
FML, sad face, I don't think it's mutual
What should I do, should I go on as usual?
I'm not sure I can, but I know there's no use
being open and truthful
Oh to be jealous, heartbroken and youthful

Help! My mind is a mess
My life is an island of stress
Of late I've been slightly obsessed
With the shape and the size of my flesh
I'm afraid that I might be depressed
Wait let me try some deep breaths
Let me count all the ways in which
I have been blessed
It's always such an effort even getting to one
Oh what inexpressible fun
It is to be emotionally delicate and young

Nobody knows the trouble I'm in
Today my favourite teacher found out
I've been cutting my skin
I've literally never ever felt so embarrassed
My Dad loves me so much
I think now he feels like a failure
Have any of you ever clocked that
shame has a flavour?
God I hate that taste more than mushrooms

My best friend since primary school is kind of
homophobic and he doesn't know I'm gay
How do I tell him? What the …k' am I gonna say?

My doctor says I'm thin but I feel fat
Any tips on how I might begin
to try and deal with that?
I dunno how to level with the adults in my life
I know they only want me to be happy but it's like
Look, it isn't your fault you don't hear me
when you listen
The way we see the world is just different

If only there was somebody who felt
the same pains as me
Of the same age as me
on the same page as me
Who when I spoke to them
they wouldn't condescend gratingly
Someone I could vent all my problems to occasionally

Not so they could magically wave them all away
Just so they could know from experience
the truth behind the crazy things I say
And maybe they too could do with a few kind words
to help them make it through the day
And imagine if a line from me
could make them feel okay

I wish there was someone like that I could speak to
Me too. Me too. Me too. Me too. Mee Two.
You too?…
Who knew.

Yumi Sakugawa

Personal Stories.

The lived experience
of mental health.

Freddie Marriage

14

The age at which 50% of adult mental health issues are already present.
Kessler et al. (2005(

Depression.

Jamie Morrell

I remember being an extremely anxious child. The thought of volcanoes, flooding, bird flu, drowning and cancer kept me up at night and made me sick with worry. I also struggled with feelings of sadness and often cried. But nothing compared to the sadness which washed over me when I was 13-years old.

It was summer and almost overnight I found I couldn't eat or sleep. The world seemed a darker place. I had a love for badminton and athletics, but I didn't feel like playing sport any more. I began spending all my time in my bedroom with the curtains shut, staring at my laptop screen.

In the pit of my stomach there was a terrible feeling of emptiness; it was as if the life had been sucked out of me. I felt exhausted and yet I couldn't sit still. Most of all, I was confused. What was happening to me? Why did I feel this way?

I desperately wanted to tell someone, anyone, how I was feeling. But who? I thought my parents would laugh it off and blame it on hormones. I thought they'd say these were normal teenage feelings; that I was just being dramatic.

Telling somebody else about the way I felt wasn't an option – I thought that boys were meant to be strong, tough, unfeeling. I had never seen my father cry, and therefore, I assumed that men didn't cry.

I was ashamed of myself for being so weak. Whenever I cried, it was as if I was doing something forbidden. I'd close the curtains and put a pillow across my face, so I could remain undetected.

My school friends were always smiling and sailed through life without a care in the world. I couldn't possibly tell them I didn't feel like living any more. In short, I was ashamed of my sadness. I felt weak. I thought there was nobody in the world like me. I was to face this alone.

Eventually, I couldn't stand my sadness any longer and began to self-harm. One evening, my Dad came into my room and noticed the cuts on my arms. At first I lied, telling him I'd fallen through a thorn bush, but he didn't believe me.

Finally, the words slipped from my mouth: 'I feel sad'.

He couldn't believe what he was hearing. I'd always had a roof over my head and food on my plate, a large group of friends and a bright future; what could I possibly have to feel sad about?

I returned to school, where everything quickly spiralled out of control. My teachers were at a loss; why had this polite young man become a lazy, argumentative troublemaker? In the classroom, I couldn't focus for more than thirty seconds before dark thoughts clouded my mind.

I had lost all motivation to succeed. I told myself I didn't care. In reality, failure terrified me. Deadlines, exams, university, the world of work: they ruled me, paralysing me with fear.

I buried my head in the sand. I felt there was no light at the end of the tunnel. I was never going to be happy. My life would never improve. I would always be a failure. I was entirely to blame, I thought.

My parents encouraged me to go and see a doctor. My desire to get better finally outweighed my fear of being laughed at. The doctor was kind, patient and understanding. He took my complaints seriously and referred me to a service for young people with potential mental illness.

I was on the waiting list for three long, painful months, but I held on. Just knowing I had taken a step forward in the right direction was enough to make me feel better.

I remember my first counselling session. It was a dark winter evening, the room bathed in a dim light. The walls were painted sea blue, and there was a picture of the bright yellow face of a daffodil.

My therapist was a gentle, soft-spoken lady. Almost immediately, I knew this was a place I could speak freely without fear of being judged. I returned on a weekly basis. Whilst my mood did not immediately lift, I did see subtle changes.

You don't expect to feel relief when a doctor tells you that you have Major Depressive Disorder, but that was my experience. There was a simple term to describe the way I felt, to explain why I behaved the way that I did! In that short, concise medical term, I realised that I wasn't to blame for my sadness.

My parents were relieved too. Like me, they had blamed themselves. We had been living under a cloud of confusion. With a diagnosis of Major Depressive Disorder, that cloud was dispersed.

I began the slow walk to happiness. Exercise, medication, journalling, mindfulness, accepting my condition and reaching out to others has all played a part in my recovery.

Sometimes my sadness will rear its ugly head, but I now have the tools to deal with it. At 22 years old, I'm the person I always wanted to be as a teenager. I have my life in order, a wide circle of friends, and a healthy relationship with my family. So be calm and patient; you can get better, too.

If you have been affected by any of the issues discussed in this article, check out the Depression Pages in the Directory on P. 100.

Masculinity.

David Willans

Until I had kids, I never thought about what it meant to be a dad. I wish I had, especially when I was a kid because I think I would have been a better son. Not that the relationship with my dad was ever bad, or that I was an absolute terror, only occasionally. I wish I'd asked that question when I was young because I would have understood my dad more. As I've got older I've realised the importance of understanding things, because if you don't understand something, you fall back on believing what others tell you to believe. So, I want to tell you what it's like being a dad, so you can understand us more.

Us dads don't get told what it means to be a dad. We are told what it means to be a man though. That's all about strength, being in control and not showing weakness. Unfortunately, this story doesn't work. It doesn't work for men and it certainly doesn't work for dads.

For many men becoming a dad is a turning point. No longer are you your own master. You are now responsible for something that will take you to new levels of emotional extreme. You experience a love you've never felt before and it's scary.

But men, real men, aren't supposed to be afraid. We're supposed to be strong, to be in control, to not take any shit. So, when we're afraid, when things are out of control, unless we think about it, we do what we've been told to do. To be strong, to dish out discipline, to exert control. Even if what's really called for is care, compassion and understanding.

A few years ago I talked to a cabby called John about being a dad, about his son's 21st birthday party. He told me about a moment early in the evening when he was sitting with his dad. His son came up, gave him a hug and kiss, told him he loved him then bounded off to the bar. John turned to his dad and said "Do you remember what you said to me when I was 8?" Without a pause, the old man said "Yes, you went to hug me and I said 'no son, men don't hug, we shake hands'. Biggest mistake of my life."

John's childhood wasn't what he wanted it to be, because his dad was doing what he thought he should do rather than thinking for himself. Thankfully, John's trying to be different. Like John, us dads are trying, but change is hard because the idea of what it means to be a real man is so deep-rooted and the things that work for being a dad, tend to be the complete opposite of what we're told works for being a man.

Being a dad isn't really about being a man. It's about being part of a family. A bunch of human beings trying to make the best lives for themselves. We've only got a chance of doing that if we work together, if we talk more and open up, something that should be a bigger part of what it means to be a dad, but isn't. Can you help us?

David is a dad to two boys, aged nine and six. Four years ago he realised he was an angry dad, something he never wanted to be, so he set up the Being Dads website to explore what it means to be a dad to help himself and others be the best dads they can be.

Self-Harm.

Emma Davies

Got the razor from the cupboard. I drew it across my arm. Sat on the floor in the bathroom on my own. I was here again. My arm scarred from previous attempts. The blood ran from the scratches. The tissue went from white to red.

I didn't care about anything else, or my family who cared about me. All I cared about was the release, the feeling I got from cutting myself. I always came back to this dark place. Going down this dark tunnel. I didn't want to return from it.

I hid my scars from those who didn't know me well. I only showed my close family. I wore long sleeved cardigans. My mother knew something was wrong. My sister asked me to show her my arm one day. Reluctant, I said "no". She pulled up the sleeve to see my arm. Still red and sore from the last time. Shocked, she couldn't believe that I did that.

Sitting in the waiting room of the mental health centre. It smelled clinical, like bleach and steriliser. The room where I sat with the nurse was small and stuffy. It was a hot summer's day.

The nurse told my mother that she thought my self-harming was just teenage angst. My mother disagreed and said it was due to deeper issues that I hadn't dealt with yet.

The nurse told me whenever I had dark thoughts or wanted to self-harm again that I should snap a rubber band on my wrist. This helped me for some time until my demons caught up with me again.

I found myself in the bathroom again. This time I was in a relationship and things were going wrong for me. My arms red with blood. I fell on the settee, going in and out of consciousness. My boyfriend wrapped my arm in tissue and tried to soak up the blood.

The scars have healed and I haven't self-harmed for some years. My family and boyfriend have helped me through these difficult times.

Things are really good for me now and I hope to work in fashion after I complete my education. I hope to pass on my experiences to others.

I hope to help those going through the issues that I was.

If you have been affected by any of the issues discussed in this article, check out the Self-harm Pages in the Directory on P. 98.

20

The percentage of young people
who self-harm before the age of 16.
Professor David Gunnell

Eating Disorders.

Anonymous

The summer of 2015 I went away on a beach holiday to Cornwall. I had posted a couple of family pictures where we were on the beach in our bikinis on my Instagram. I didn't have an issue with this as I had a private account which only my friends could see.

A few months later I had a follow request on my Instagram from an unknown person. I opened it up to look and there was me in my bikini and an overweight celebrity, side by side. The comments were "Your celebrity twin." In the image I was a healthy weight, just on the borderline of healthy from underweight but they were calling me fat? I had numerous people commenting on my weight and I was distraught!

By December I had blocked all my friends and I was too scared of who it could be (it had to be one of my followers). I took the matter into my own hands, got the post deleted and thought I should sort out my weight! I started cutting out fat foods, sugar, then carbs and then meat, leaving me with vegetables. I started walking over 30,000 steps a day, eating one meal, until it began to be nothing.

I started losing weight and by around May my parents were worried. With bowel problems running in the family and when I did eat, getting bad IBS my parents sent me to the doctor where I was diagnosed with IBS. I was given nutrition shakes which I could tolerate with the 'illness'. I started tipping them down the sink, replacing with water and I wasn't gaining. I was still losing.

That August we went away, all inclusive food! I was watched so I started eating and strangely enough I only gained half a stone in two weeks of me scoffing my face! My family thought nothing of it! When I got back in September, I restricted again and lost a lot more. In December my parents had clocked I wasn't eating so started weighing me weekly to make sure I was gaining. I would gain and lose. One time I lost half a stone in under a week so my parents just got me into the doctors that January 2017.

The doctor there diagnosed me with Anorexia Nervosa. I was sent right away to a specialist hospital and was checked out. The weight I was, was very dangerous and they were considering inpatient. There wasn't any beds so I stayed outpatient. At the time I was determined to stay outpatient and gain the weight.

A few months later I had gained weight but got very depressed. I was caught trying to buy something which I was going to commit suicide with, and Mum took me to the children's hospital straight away. From then on I was on 1:1 watch and forced to eat and not to harm myself.

I started eating and gaining more and as soon as I was alone and left to my own devices I started purging every bit of food I ate. This made me lose weight and they were concerned. I denied I was purging and they left it at that.

Continued on page 18

14

The average age for the onset of an eating disorder.
McManus et al. (2016)

Scarlet Evans

Continued from page 16

Talking.
Dr Pooky Knightsmith

A couple of weeks later I had been in and out of hospital taking overdoses and having potassium (due to the purging). It got to June and I ran away from home to again take my own life. The police came and I admitted to purging, but in July I again tried to take my own life. However, that was the last time.

I have started using the MeeTwo app now. It's a great way to express anything without embarrassment or being judged. Somewhere where you can be you, receiving amazing support from the whole community.

I am now self-harm free and nearly purge free. I have become a healthy weight and I actually am content in my body. Although I've been through a tough battle I feel I've come through the long dark tunnel and I can finally start to live my life again. I may struggle but it can never be as bad as it has been!

Young people with mental health difficulties can be hard to reach and we often end up pushing them away in our efforts to draw them closer.

Here are ten nuggets of advice, directly from young people who've been in need of help.

If you have been affected by any of the issues discussed in this article, check out the Body Image Pages in the Directory on P. 66

If you are having thoughts of suicide, or are worried about a friend, call either of these numbers.
Papyrus Youth Hopeline: 0800 068 41 41
The Samaritans: 116 123

Dr Pooky Knightsmith is a passionate ambassador for youth mental health. Her enthusiasm is backed up both by a PhD in child and adolescent mental health and her own lived experience of PTSD, anorexia, self-harm, anxiety and depression.

Focus on listening

"She listened, and I mean REALLY listened. She didn't interrupt me or ask me to explain myself or anything, she just let me talk and talk and talk. I had been unsure about talking to anyone but I knew quite quickly that I'd chosen the right person to talk to and that it would be a turning point."

Don't talk too much

"Sometimes it's hard to explain what's going on in my head – it doesn't make a lot of sense and I've kind of gotten used to keeping myself to myself. But just 'cos I'm struggling to find the right words doesn't mean you should help me. Just keep quiet, I'll get there in the end."

Drop everything

"I knew he was taking me seriously because the first thing he did was to sit me down quietly whilst he called the head teacher to arrange for someone else to teach his next lesson. That sort of scared me but more than that it made me realise that he actually cared about what I was going to tell him and that he really wanted to help."

Don't pretend to understand

"I think all teachers got taught on some course somewhere to say "I understand how that must feel' the moment you open up. YOU DON'T – don't even pretend to, it's not helpful, it's insulting."

Acknowledge how hard it is to discuss issues

"Talking about my bingeing for the first time was the hardest thing I ever did. When I was done talking, X looked me in the eye and said, 'That must have been really tough' – he was right, it was, but it meant so much that he realised what a big deal it was for me."

Offer support

"I was worried how she'd react, but my mum just listened then said, 'How can I support you?' – no one had asked me that before and it made me realise that she cared, and between us we thought of some really practical things she could do to help me stop self-harming."

Don't be afraid to make eye contact

"She was so disgusted by what I told her that she couldn't bear to look at me."

Persevere

"I think she thought I would never open up. It was probably after she'd outstretched a hand of support about eight times that I finally began to talk, falteringly. If she hadn't have kept trying and trying I'd probably still be sitting in that deep pit of depression now."

Don't assume that an apparently negative response is actually a negative response

"The anorexic voice in my head was telling me to push help away so I was saying no. But there was a tiny part of me that wanted to get better. I just couldn't say it out loud or else I'd have to punish myself."

Never break your promises

"If you say you'll be there, be there. If you say you'll keep it a secret, keep it a secret. Whatever you say you'll do, you have to do or else the trust we've built in you will be smashed to smithereens. And never lie. Just be honest. If you're going to tell someone just be upfront about it, we can handle that, what we can't handle is having our trust broken."

Male Anorexia.

Sam Pollen

If you ask Hollywood, everyone who develops an eating disorder looks pretty much the same. There are dozens of movies about The Pretty, Popular Girl With A Dark Secret. She's a model, or a ballerina, or a cheerleader. She's under huge pressure to pass her exams, get into drama school, find a boyfriend. She's deeply unhappy – but in the end, everything works out because this is Hollywood, and we all love a happy ending.

I'm sure lots of people fit this stereotype, but many more don't. Right now, in the UK, 1.25 million people are living with an eating disorder. These people are young and old. Rich and poor. Male, female, and non-binary, and of all backgrounds and ethnicities.

Some of them are obviously thin, but many are not, because you can have an eating disorder with any body shape. There are anorexic accountants out there, and bulimic builders. You almost certainly know someone who has an eating disorder, even if you don't know that you do.

I was 12 when I was first diagnosed with anorexia. I wasn't under any pressure. I didn't dance (trust me, you don't want to see me dance). I had a supportive family around me, and friends, and everything was . . . fine. Until it wasn't.

Movies tend to do a good job of communicating some parts of an eating disorder. The arguments. The throwing up. The drama. But they don't show you the everyday reality.

In my case, the everyday reality was this: I sat in my bedroom, and stared at the walls. It turns out, once you take friends and food out of your life, there isn't a lot to do.

I ran a lot, until the doctors stopped me from doing that. Then I mostly just sat there, and thought about the food I wasn't eating, and counted down the calories I knew I was burning just by being alive. It wouldn't have made a great movie.

The truth is, I was dying. That sounds dramatic, but it's just honest: anorexia has the highest mortality rate of any mental health condition, one that's similar to some cancers. I was sitting there, doing nothing, and it was slowly killing me.

Eventually, I got better. What helped me through my eating disorder were an extremely patient and supportive family, a few very kind teachers, the NHS, and time. Lots of time. There was and is no magic bullet, I'm afraid; eating disorder recovery is weird and unpredictable. There are false starts, days of horror, days of happiness, days of frustration. For some people, it takes months. For others, it may take decades.

Continued on page 22

Ellen Pearson

The age at which most boys are admitted to hospital for an eating disorder.
Health and Social Care Information Centre

13

Continued from page 20

Sadly, that 1.25 million number is on the rise. It may already be a gross underestimate. Why? What are we getting wrong? Should we blame the media: stick-thin women in magazines, body-shaming, men with ripped abs and protein powders to sell?

Is it because the NHS is overstretched, underfunded, and chronically short of the exact kinds of people – counsellors, clinical psychologists – who can help? Do we blame Instagram? Snapchat? Facebook?

What about a school system that makes young people jump through more and more hoops, exam after exam, to fill league tables and UCAS forms? It's all of those. That's the trouble with real-life mental health, as opposed to Hollywood mental health: it isn't simple, and there isn't always a happy ending.

But looking back, one thing I know would've helped me is stories – stories of other people who were maybe a bit like me, and who'd made it through the other side. Rationally, I guess I knew these people existed. But I never really believed it, because I never heard their stories.

That's why this handbook matters. That's why MeeTwo matters. That's why I'm writing this: to send up a flare. I'm not saying I understand everything you're going through. But I understand a bit of it. And here I am, on the other side, ready to talk. And I promise you: there are plenty of other people, with different backgrounds and different experiences, ready to do the same.

Every day, all kinds of people develop eating disorders. But the flip side is: every day, all kinds of people recover from eating disorders. They might not all make great movies, but there are millions of happy endings out there.

Samuel Pollen is now a writer. He comes from Cheshire but lives in London. His debut teen novel, which is all about his experience with anorexia will be published next year. You can find out more on his website: samuelpollen.com.

The Year I Didn't Eat, will be published by ZunTold in April 2019.

If you have been affected by any of the issues discussed in this article, check out the Body Image Pages in the Directory on P. 66

The number of young people aged 11-15 who miss school primarily due to bullying.
The Anti-Bulllying Alliance

Mulberry UTC

Bullying.

Anonymous

I was a part of a lovely group for most of my time at secondary school. We weren't the coolest kids walking the corridors, but we were happy. In year nine, a new girl who seemed nice enough appeared to take a shine to me. I had never had a BEST friend, so I leapt at the opportunity to have a close friendship with her. During this time, I didn't realise how much I was distancing myself from my oldest friends, my truest friends.

When two of my friends started to fall out, my new friend egged them on. She formed a close bond with one of the girls whilst telling her untrue rumours about the other. You'd think I'd be most concerned with the untrue rumours, but no. I just couldn't believe my 'best friend' was betraying me and spending her time with someone else. It seems stupid now, but at the time it really hurt me.

I never said anything mean but I am guilty of not telling the other girls what my 'best friend' was doing. She was mixing the batter for a cake of lies and hurt.

Eventually it all came out. The evening of the first day of year ten was one of the worst of my life. My 'best friend' told me that everyone hated us. In the blink of an eye, I'd lost all my friends. I struggled to get my head round this. What had I said or done? Then I realised, because I was in such a close-knit 'friendship' with this girl, they had assumed I was just like her; I'd lost my individualism and was looked at as a sheep, a follower of this girl. I was no better than she was. At this point, it would have been the sensible time for me to approach the girls and tell them I'd never said anything horrible, but I was too worried they wouldn't believe me. Instead, I apologised for something I had never done. People were shocked when they found out the girl they thought was 'so lovely' was in fact a bi***.

The messages started rolling in from the girls. Even if they thought I'd said horrible things about them, the messages were the worst thing I'd ever read; the ding signifying I had a new message sent fear sweeping over me.

Being hated by all of the girls might not have been so bad if I wasn't in a form with them; I was completely isolated. I dreaded going to school, feeling sick to my stomach every morning. Inevitably, this resulted in me taking loads of days off, only to sit in my room endlessly crying about how tough my life was. As a coping mechanism, I bought a massive calendar and whenever I got home after having a bad day at school - which was most days, I would cross off the date.

Looking back, I'm not sure how I didn't realise how bad she was. She was horrible about other people, but she was covertly horrible to ME. She would find sneaky ways of making me feel bad about myself through ridiculous means. If I texted her that I was going to be late to meet or I wasn't in school, she would send an icy reply and be cruel for the rest of the day.

The situation gradually resolved, but I lived the rest of my days at school in fear. My message to anyone going through a toxic friendship is get out of it; there's no point surrounding yourself with horrible people.

Self-Injury.

Issy MacLennan

I remember distinctly the time self-harm was starting to be an issue. I was in Year nine, and only 13 years old,. It is horrible to think about that now when I realise how young I was. Like many 13-year-olds, I had a Tumblr account, where I started to see images of self-harm.

Back then there were barely any regulations for this kind of thing. People I followed spoke about how they felt sad, depressed etc, and I felt what they were saying related to me.

I found it hard to speak about my issues, so instead I decided that harming myself would help, because that's what these people online were doing and they said it worked for them.

Self-harm is a coping strategy for people with overwhelming/distressing thoughts and feelings. The act itself is harming and injuring your body, or non-lethal overdoses. The most common way is cutting, pinching, banging and burning the skin.

I should've spoken to my parents about how I was feeling, but I didn't, and so this 'coping mechanism' I developed continued for four years whenever I felt stressed. Eventually my parents found out. The best help for me was beginning to open up about how I was feeling and from there I eventually began to understand the state of my mental health and how to improve it.

It's been five years since I last self-harmed and earlier this year I was diagnosed with depression. If I had reached out to someone, such as my parents, this probably would've been sorted a lot sooner and I would've received the treatment that

I needed, but I wasn't aware of who I could talk to and didn't think anything could help me.

A friend who wished to remain anonymous had a similar experience. An event in her life was the trigger, and then it became a serious issue. "I did it because it felt like a cathartic release from everything I felt at the time. It built up and up for so long and when other people caught wind of the fact I was doing it, they told me they did it too."

She self-harmed from the age of 12 until she was 18. "I never did this for attention, I want to make this clear, but when other people who self-harm find out you do, it sort of turns into a competition about who does it most and who is more damaged or sad, based on how much you've hurt yourself.'

This seems very common, and almost drives you to it more, like you have to prove to yourself how you are feeling. She explained what eventually began helping her: "You have to try and help yourself even if you don't want to. Harming yourself is not a good coping mechanism and is so dangerous. Seek out help in a friend or a family member, from a doctor if needs be. But don't continue to damage yourself."

According to the Mental Health Foundation, roughly two students in a typical secondary school classroom will have self-harmed at some point. If you are struggling with this issue, please see a doctor because your mental health is the most important thing and when you're young you don't necessarily know how to look after it.

70

The percentage of young people in the UK who experience mental health problems but can't access appropriate interventions at a sufficiently early age.
Mental Health Foundation, 2015

Scarlet Evans

The percentage of young people who have experienced suicidal thoughts at some point.

25

Alexander Kireev

Suicide.

Anonymous

I am extremely lucky to live the life that I do; I live in a loving home with a family who would do anything for me and I have the most amazing friends. The first 15 years of my life are full of happy memories. I was a child who was always positive and smiling and yet I have spent the last year of my life battling depression.

It started in year 11 before my GCSE mocks. I had always worked hard at school and I was predicted all A's and A*'s, but I got very stressed about my upcoming exams and I started to find work a lot harder. My passion for sport disappeared and I started dreading it. I felt really down and some nights I would cry myself to sleep. Other nights I wouldn't sleep at all. It was really confusing.

One of my teachers told me I needed mental health support, but I hated the idea of talking to a stranger. I couldn't understand my own feelings and emotions and I didn't know anything about mental health. I remember doing lots of depression tests online at the time, so I think that subconsciously I knew that I might have depression. I just didn't want it to be true.

After a whole term of feeling like that, I thought the Christmas holidays might help but it was worse. All I remember thinking was 'if I can't be happy on Christmas Day, how can I ever be happy at all?' I was meant to be revising for my mocks but every attempt ended in tears. I began to feel very anxious about my lack of concentration and I was terrified of the idea of failing my exams.

When I got back to school and sat in the first exam, I opened the paper and tears started pouring down my face. I walked out of the hall in front of my whole year, just 10 minutes into the exam. That was the moment I realised I needed help and I finally agreed to go to counselling.

At first I hated it, and it didn't help at all, but it did help me to understand my feelings a bit more. At school, I still couldn't concentrate and in my lowest moments, I started self-harming. I kept this a secret for a long time because I couldn't bear the thought of someone finding out.

I was worried that people would judge me and that it would upset people, so I just hid my scars. By half-term I was hardly doing any work at school and my teacher asked me directly whether I self-harmed. I tried to hide it, but she could tell I was lying.

My mum was called and I had to go to see my GP. I was terrified but the doctor told me I have endogenous depression and in an odd way, this was a relief to me because I could now understand my feelings and get the help I needed to get better. I was referred to CAMHS and saw a psychiatrist every month or so, as well as seeing the school counsellor weekly.

My relationship with my parents got really bad. I had this blockage that prevented me from talking to them. Even if I wanted to, I just couldn't. Home became somewhere I hated to be.

I couldn't talk to anyone there and I spent the whole time in my bedroom alone. By that stage it was a constant battle every morning to just get out of bed.

One night, I felt so lost in my own home, that I wrapped up warm and ran away. My dad and brother were driving around for hours whilst I sat in a shed, about a mile away from home, crying. I know it was a very stupid thing to do but I was so mixed up.

My teacher rang me and left a voice mail, and I called her back. She came to pick me up and drove me home, and we had a long chat with my parents. I hated every single second of it but I learnt one thing: running away isn't a solution.

The next day the GP prescribed antidepressants for me. I was hopeful that they would help, but I was also scared to think that my happiness now depended on medication. I found being at school easier than being at home because I could be around my friends and I could talk to my teacher, or my counsellor.

By the end of term I really thought I was on the up, but I was very anxious about the holidays. I still couldn't speak to my parents and at home, my mood dropped and I felt like I was back to square one. I hardly left my bedroom and stayed in bed pretty much all day, every day. I only came downstairs for meal times, but my appetite gradually disappeared.

At one point I was only eating a couple of carrot sticks a day. I was going downhill fast. I had horrible thoughts and started questioning the point of my life.

One day I went bowling with my friends, which was good, but it triggered some dangerous thoughts. I started asking myself the question, 'if this is meant to be fun and I can't enjoy it, then how am I meant to cope doing work and other stuff?'

That day, I decided I had had enough. I bought some medicine and went home. I had decided I couldn't live my life any more. I didn't have a particular wish to die, but I didn't care if I did. I was broken. I stayed up until 4am and overdosed, but I felt so ill that I couldn't bear it and I woke my parents. I spent the next two days on a drip in hospital. It was the worst two days of my life because I was so sick. The whole time my parents took turns to sit in the chair next to my hospital bed and I felt so guilty for putting them through this.

A week later I was back at school. I completed my GCSE's, but I wasn't eating. It got to the point where I was counting calories obsessively and eating a maximum of 200 calories each day. At my lowest weight, I was 15 kg lighter than I am today. My weight was the one thing I thought I could control, but by then, it was controlling me.

My weight was measured by the school health centre every week and my psychiatrist told me I had one week to turn it around, otherwise I would end up in hospital. I was scared of the fact that I wasn't in control of my eating, but I really wanted to get better.

The turning point for me was being allowed to help out in the nursery school between my exams. I absolutely love children and it made me so happy. At lunchtime, all the children and adults ate together and I had no choice but to eat. So I did. I ate a proper meal! It was not easy and I had to face huge feelings of guilt afterwards, but I did it, and it was like something had clicked. I felt happy again.

I still have bad days, but I'm learning how to cope with them. I am now attending 95% of my lessons and my relationship with my family is better too.

I have also started using MeeTwo and it has helped me so much. I can post my thoughts, feelings, worries, emotions whenever I need to, and get advice from young people suffering from mental health issues back. It really is amazing, and allows young people to offload and help each other. It helps me view my experience with mental health, as horrible as it was, as a positive thing now, because I can help others who are going through the same thing and that makes me feel great.

I have only used MeeTwo since I started recovering from depression, but I wish I'd had it earlier. During my lowest moments, even making a post expressing how I was feeling would have really helped me.

MeeTwo is a life-saver.

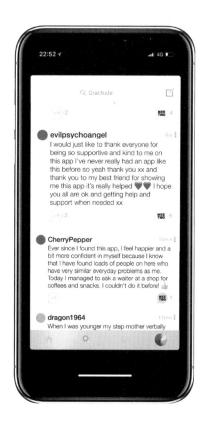

Panic Attacks.

Bethany Thomas

When I am feeling anxious, or if I am having a panic attack, music is my anchor. I have a playlist of the songs that calm me down so that I can easily access them when I feel anxious or panicked.

Another tip is to make playlists of classical music, or calming sounds like rain, or coffee-shop noise. I also find that having noise cancelling headphones helps because it allows me to block everything around me out to focus on myself.

Poppy has panic attacks too. I asked her about her experience. She said, "I've been having panic attacks for roughly five years now and only recently have I found that practising mindfulness and meditation combined with natural remedies in my day-to-day life actually gives me the tools to be like, 'this is happening, here's how to deal with it'."

The natural remedies she uses are things such as crystals, lavender, ylang-ylang and sage and she also drinks herbal teas like camomile to help her be calm. Poppy also recommended using the app Headspace for meditation.

Mind.org describes anxiety as "what we feel when we are worried, tense or afraid — particularly about things that are about to happen, or which we think could happen in the future".

Panic attacks come in different ways, not just hyperventilation (rapid, shallow breathing). Panic attacks can also feel like a pounding or racing heartbeat, feeling faint, dizzy or light-headed, sweating, trembling or shaking, or nausea.

After a panic attack, try to listen to your body. If you feel tired, take a 30-minute nap. Taking a walk and getting fresh air is an easy way to distract and relax yourself. If you're comfortable doing so, talk to someone about how you're feeling, whether it is a friend, or family member that you trust. If you don't feel like speaking to someone, keep a journal and write out how you are feeling. This will help you track your mood and allow you to figure out what triggers you, if you are not already aware.

Megan also suffers from anxiety and panic attacks. She says, "I'm not great at dealing with them alone. I'd say the most important thing is grounding - maybe feeling a familiar surface or texture or being with a familiar person speaking to you. Getting your breathing on track is really important for me and that's where another person is most helpful in guiding you."

There are many tips online about the best ways to steady your breathing. Sitting down and picking things that you can name, or count in your head, will shift your focus and calm you down. One final tip, avoid caffeine when you can because it affects stress hormones and can make your heart beat faster, leading to further feelings of panic or anxiousness.

5

The number of teenagers
in any classroom who are
living with anxiety.
Anxiety UK

Treatment.

Tayla Kruger

If you have been affected by any of the issues discussed in this article, check out the Therapy Pages in the Directory on P. 94

As someone who's faced overcoming their anxiety disorder, I know how exhausting it can be to find the most effective treatment for yourself.

The process of trial and error isn't ideal for those of us who just want a fast solution so we can get on with our lives without being held back by mental illness. After talking with my doctor about all the different factors of both, I decided to go for medication as a way of tackling my anxiety. Overall, I had a positive experience with it and after feeling a bit of nausea and drowsiness in the first two weeks, I started to see a positive change in my mood, as well as feeling more motivated and optimistic about things that used to stress me.

There's no sure way of knowing which treatment is right for you, so it's important to take everything into consideration. For some, therapy or drugs alone provide a huge amount of relief, sometimes using both therapies simultaneously increases the chances of a full recovery. Recovery is a process and everyone's different. Just because a certain treatment works for someone else it doesn't mean it'll work for you. No matter which way you decide to go, you need to put self-care first and utilise all the support around you from friends and family.

The two main routes that people choose to take are talk therapy (also known as psychotherapy, or medication, but both options have pros and cons. It mostly comes down to the 'nature or nurture' argument. Does mental illness stem from what we've faced in our lives and our experiences, or is it because of our brain chemistry? Scientists have been asking this question for decades and still haven't come to a definitive decision. It's widely accepted that genetics does play a part in our mental health, but so does the environment and what happens around us.

Talk Therapy Pros: It can be a good way to deal with depression, anxiety, bipolar and many other mental illnesses. A good therapist can help you recognise your feelings and cope with them in healthy ways. Some might prefer this over taking medication alone because it gives you insight into what the problem stems from.

Talk Therapy Cons: It normally takes longer to see results so it can feel discouraging at first. Therapy on the NHS can also involve being on a waiting list for up to six months before you can get treated. It can be a frustrating process, especially when you want immediate help.

Antidepressants Pros: Drugs target the brain and SSRIs such as fluoxetine which is used to treat depression, prevents serotonin, the chemical that makes you happy, from leaving your brain.

Antidepressants Cons: Some people think of medication as a temporary solution and while it may make you feel better, it doesn't go to the root of the issue like therapy does. Another thing you'll understand if you've ever been prescribed antidepressants is the seemingly never-ending list of possible side effects. They can even make your symptoms worse for the first two weeks but after that you should start to feel an improvement - if not, it's important that you tell your doctor so they can find another remedy for you.

70,000

The number of people under the age of 18 in the UK taking antidepressants.

NHS data obtained by The Times newspaper, 2018

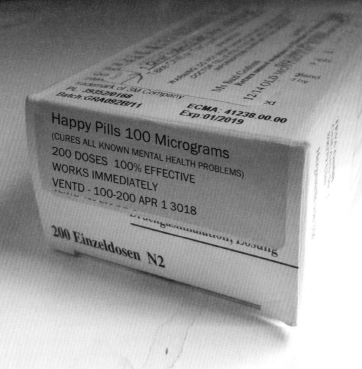

Trademark of 3M Company
PL. 38352/0168
Batch GRA092B/11

ECMA · 41238.00.00
Exp:01/2019

Happy Pills 100 Micrograms
(CURES ALL KNOWN MENTAL HEALTH PROBLEMS)
200 DOSES 100% EFFECTIVE
WORKS IMMEDIATELY
VENTD - 100-200 APR 1 3018

200 Einzeldosen N2

CAMHS.

Anonymous

Find out more about CAMHS in the Therapy pages of the Directory on page 94 and read Emma Selby's 'CAMHS Explained' interview on page B20

I'm 16 years old and I was diagnosed with the illness from 15 years old. I was bullied in the past for all my high school experience except the last 2 years because it's now been stopped because I told the teacher. When I was bullied the boys called me names and threw things like paper, pens, plastic at me. It made me sad.

The reason I got ill was because I felt very insecure about the way I looked and felt and I wanted to change the way I looked, by controlling what I eat and how much. The school noticed my behaviour change dramatically over that year and I became very ill from my mental health because I wanted to be a certain weight.

The teachers were concerned so they told my mum to make an appointment with my GP and that's what she did. I had blood tests and they came back deficient in B12 so I was put on B12 supplements and I am still on them to this day.

After that, my doctor referred me to the NHS's Child and Adolescent Mental Health Services (CAMHS) because of my behaviour in school and towards my family. When I was at CAMHS the first time I felt scared, sad, and worried. I had quite a lot of mixed emotions. When I got support from CAMHS, I didn't know what to expect and I was very shy and nervous. As the sessions went on I talked more and explained to her what's been happening and how I'm feeling. I still get support from them now.

The counselling I had helped a little bit, from being able to talk to someone about the way I feel and what I was thinking. Also it was the advice that my counsellor gave me that helped me and I felt less lonely. What my school did to help and support me was letting me go somewhere if I feel sad or angry in lessons and to talk to me if I was sad or thinking bad thoughts.

What makes me feel better is the support my Mum and Nan are giving me, and having CAMHS to talk to and my school supporting me through it all. What makes me feel worse is having arguments with parents and being lonely at school, which happens.

The CAMHS's team that recommended me the MeeTwo app was the Chelmsford team. The lady told me about it because of my self-harming problems. The app MeeTwo helps me see what others are going through and it helps me feel better when I give advice to others. I like this app a lot because everyone supports each other and I can relate myself to what others have gone through and what I have gone through.

My ambition for the future is to go to college and do an early years course so then I can work with children at nurseries/playgroups. Which I would love because I love helping children and creating bonds with them. I would tell other people in my situation to try your best and take your time. Take every five minutes as it comes. Don't stress and don't worry about life. It is not worth it. You can do anything in life if you put your mind to it.

MY HEAD IS SO FULL

HOPE

61

The percentage of GP referrals to CAMHS that are rejected.
Pulse GP News Website, 2015

Body Image.

Sadia Ali

Looks are important, we all know. We want to wake up in the morning and like what we see. We want to be beautiful. But who defines what beautiful is? Is it our friends, people at school, or even social media?

Everyday we scroll through Instagram and are hit with thousands of pictures that tell us the 'right way' to be beautiful. Or so you think. The cheat code to beauty is, as clichéd as it sounds, confidence and a whole lot of faith in yourself. This is coming from someone who went through the hell of secondary school and came out the best version of myself and armed with unending confidence.

It's easy to get lost in social media when you're still finding yourself. Many people online only show their best bits and a lot of times even mislead us in how they achieved their looks. But the truth is many of these people have gone under the knife.

So how can we aspire to look like someone who doesn't even look like themselves? It is easier (and cheaper) to just love yourself. Know that you are beautiful and unique and don't root your worth in how other people see you.

Women come in a million different shades, sizes and shapes. Some of the most beautiful women in the world don't fit in to these so-called beauty standards. Take, for example, the gorgeous American model Ashley Graham or the radiant actress Lupita Nyong'o.

Be Your Best Self

Make your mark and be your own brand of beauty. Look to the women around you and use them as role models, like your mum, sisters and cousins or even teachers.

List all the things you're good at. Are you kind, funny, the fastest in class?

Focus on all the things you love about yourself. Got beautiful hair? Well take extra care of it by making sure it's conditioned, moisturised and brushed.

Beauty begins from within, but we can sure make it work for ourselves by taking care of it.

Real beauty is the belief in yourself so take pride in being different. I, and all the women and girls in my life don't fit in to standards of beauty, but that makes us more beautiful. So be you, beautiful.

Check out the Dove Self-Esteem Project and the Free Being Me campaign on the Dove website. It has lots of resources and activities that can help you if you're struggling with your body image, from activities to do at home or even workshops you can attend to give you a boost.

If you have been affected by any of the issues discussed in this article, check out the Body Image Pages in the Directory on P. 66

2.5

The percentage prevalence of body dysmorphic disorder.
International OCD Federation

Body hair.

Fatima Batool

nhs.uk/conditions/polycystic-ovary-syndrome-pcos/
nhs.uk/conditions/hirsutism/
skinsupport.org.uk/conditions-details/hirsutism
hirsutism.blogspot.co.uk/

Threading, waxing, lasering, an epilator and a whole lot of PAIN. Removing facial and body hair can be a real struggle… but maybe there's a solution that doesn't cause the amount of pain hair removal causes: acceptance and embracing oneself. All of us will deal with body and facial hair at some point in our lives.

Some us will have more than others, some will have hair which is coarser than others, and some will have hair grow back quicker than they can scream REMOVE. While there may be medical reasons as to why we deal with excess hair, such as Polycystic Ovary Syndrome (PCOS), for others it may just be because they are naturally hairy. And that's okay.

PCOS affects every one in 10 women and influences how a woman's ovaries work. Features of PCOS include irregular periods, high levels of male hormones and polycystic ovaries. There are many symptoms such as oily skin and acne, thinning hair and hair loss from your head, excessive hair growth (hirsutism), irregular periods or no periods at all, weight gain and difficulty getting pregnant. However, some women don't experience any symptoms. It is important to go and seek medical advice from a professional if you think you may have PCOS.

Coming from a south Asian background where many of my family members are hairy, it is something that I had to deal with growing up. It was a major insecurity. As I grew older, I noticed I had more facial hair and decided to go and do something about it.

My mum advised me to go to a hair removal shop with her and try threading. Threading can be painful, but your hair takes longer to grow than after waxing. But threading my hair just wasn't something I had the time to do every two to four weeks. I just didn't want to go through the pain again and again, and it can be expensive when you're threading your eyebrows, upper lip and a whole lot more. Whilst waxing is faster, it can also be just as painful and still costs money, plus it can cause spots to appear and be harmful to your skin done frequently.

Waking up every morning, looking into a mirror and using a whole lot of makeup and everything you can to hide your hair is time consuming and not a nice feeling. But, I was sure I couldn't be the only one going through this. The insecurity I felt, thinking every person I cross paths with when leaving my home was staring at the thick hairs upon my face. So, I decided to Google all things to do with facial hair… and it was the best decision I could have made.

I found that so many women go through this issue, and there are so many support groups and forums out there to help. Not only did I find that many women who went to the doctor about their excess hair found they had a hormonal problem or PCOS, some went and found they had nothing wrong and it's just one of those things.

Billie

10

The percentage of women who suffer from polycistic ovary syndrome.
Brady, Mousa & Mousa (2009)

Some women used a medical cream prescribed by their GP to help, and some just decided to embrace it by accepting that it's a natural part of life for many women, regardless of ethnic group.

Syeda Iftikhar has dealt with insecurities and esteem issues about her hair problems. "Having hair on parts of your face you don't want hair to be on can definitely be a real downer," she says, "especially when going to high school or work and being around a lot of people. But I have learned that it's not the end of the world and there are bigger issues to worry about.

When you're going through an issue like a family member passing away, or meeting someone who accepts you for you, you just forget about it and learn to live with it. I don't obsess over it any more because the older I got, the more I learned to just love myself for who I am, to stop trying to meet society's expectations and change myself for others, and to spend more time with people who already do love me, for me.

"When I want to remove my hair, I will, but if I don't feel like it, or don't want to, I won't. That's the way I deal with it now, and it feels good."

I have learned to just remove the amount of hair so I feel comfortable, where I can still be in my happy place and not care what others are thinking because it doesn't mean that you're less of a woman.

To all the girls out there struggling with body and facial hair issues – just be you and embrace it, because those who matter won't be bothered about it, and the ones who get bothered about your body hair shouldn't matter.

If you have been affected by any of the issues discussed in this article, check out the Body Image Pages in the Directory on P. 66

Anonymous Poem
Mulberry UTC

Stories,
experiences
locked in your mind.
The key thrown,
for someone else to find.
The pain, the agony,
too much to bear.
Yet they insert the key,
try to show that they care.

You let them in,
but why do you regret?
Take the key back,
ask them to forget?
You don't trust yourself,
so why trust them?
You've been broken before,
why not again?

So hide the key,
in a place unknown.
And maybe then,
they'll leave you alone.
But that's not what you want,
so what do you do?
Bring the key back? Uncover the truth?

You want them to stay and help you grow.
You want them to try, but how far can they go?
You think you've tried, but is it enough?
You need a friend, one you can trust.

They'll never understand the emotions you face.
So you feel too alone and out of place.
You'll just have to stay alone
to win this fight.
You'll be fine…
but is this
decision
right?

Scarlet Evans

Friendship.

Kitty Drake

Female friendship might be the most under-appreciated cause of mental illness. We've started to understand the emotional violence of love, lust and family relationships – but we still think of friendship as a kind of unadulterated good. Slightly unhinged in itself: I still define myself by the intensity of my relationship with a group of girls I met when we were eleven. All my crimes of passion – intense jealousy, rage and angst – have been because of those girls.

And if my friendships with them were to break down, I'd take it as a personal failure – (as females we're conditioned to take most relationship breakdown as a personal failure). What me and my friends don't like to admit is we might not be making each other particularly happy.

Part of that is because my friendships – like many female friendships – are built on shared pain. Our closeness is predicated on trading confidences: picking together over an unrequited love, a failure, or a mutual hate. This is what makes female friendship so intimate and precious, but at the same time threaded with the potentiality for trauma.

Dubbed 'co-rumination' by psychologist Amanda Rose, this endless reopening of an old wound is proven to trigger depression. Rose found that while girls who co-ruminated enjoyed closer relationships with their friends, they were also more susceptible to emotional disorders. You can also get to a point where the only thing you have in common with your friend any more is that wound. Without quite admitting it, I've found myself willing a friend to stay rejected,

stay resentful, stay struggling, just so we'll have something to talk about. It's a delicious feeling, being miserable together. But it gets suffocating.

The story we tell one another about ourselves – over and over again – acquires a nice ring to it. Keeping the same friends, rare and wonderful in many ways, also runs the risk of trapping you in one role. If you're the 'frigid' one, or the 'anxious' one, or the one who's always there to support, you can end up self-defining as an adult using labels that were thought up at school when you were all still children. Turning points in life – recovering from an eating disorder; acknowledging your sexuality – become almost impossible when you're still trying, in an essential way, to live up to the person you were 15 years ago.

Letting go of a friendship, according to author and psychologist Carol Topolski, "requires a kind of mourning". But it's pain that's not often talked about. It's far more shameful to have a friend leave you than a lover: wondering what you did wrong feels more personal; asking yourself whether you demanded too much, were too desperate. Finding out who you are outside the group can be very lonely – it feels like a part of you has died. But it also moves you forward. Friendships should be raw, you should demand something romantic and intrinsic of one another. But sometimes trying to be everything to one another means erasing significant parts of yourself. Or, if you're me: becoming a possessive witch. Maybe the thing we weren't taught as girls growing up is that you can also survive on your own.

8.7

The number (out of ten) that young people aged 11 to 15 rate their "happiness with friends." In 1995 this figure was exactly the same as it is today.
The Good Childhood Report 2018

The number of single parent families with dependent children in the UK.
Gingerbread: the charity supporting single parent families

2,000,000

Scarlet Evans

Divorce.

Byron Jamar Terry

Although I don't usually talk too much about my personal life, in order to understand where I am today, I have to take it back to my childhood.

Growing up, I would consider myself as a happy kid for the most part. Almost spoiled in a way. My parents didn't necessarily go overboard with stuff, but I loved going outside, playing with toys, video games, sports and more. I did it all. Just like any normal kid.

However, moving a lot steadily started to become more of the norm. I moved so much as a kid and even a teenager that it began to really wear me down. It was really difficult for me to deal with it. It'd be really stressful at times but I got through it. It seemed as if every day I'd pass somewhere else that I had lived at some point.

When my mother and father got a divorce things began to change. Although they told me it wasn't my fault, the transition from family life to a single parent home was difficult. Often times, I took the brunt of it.

My escape was football. In between those lines, I could be immune from all outside noise. I would get lost in the game, and for those two hours each week, I was free. Yet inevitably, the game always has to end. Often times, after games I would kind of sit around and hang out. I'd talk to other people's parents and families. It was difficult without both of my parents being there. Seeing everybody happy with their mums and dads was honestly heartbreaking.

My mum would come up to me and congratulate me but it just felt different without my biological father or even my step-father at the time, just not being around as much.

As a football player, you're taught to never reveal weakness, and I took that notion to heart. I began to become increasingly distant from my teammates. There'd be times at practice where you would find me by myself head down. Silent. Totally removed from the equation.

Usually if I didn't play well, I'd be really down on myself. Sometimes I'd feel really alone and be by myself a whole lot. I could be at a party having an enjoyable time then a few minutes later be sitting by myself and not talk to anyone. People would ask me what's wrong if I'm just quiet, but I would be reluctant to tell them what's wrong. I guess that just comes with being depressed.

It got so bad, I began contemplating suicidal thoughts. Feeling so incredibly helpless, I finally decided to confide in my mum for the very first time. Shortly after that I started seeing a therapist and taking medication. I still take prescribed medication.

I've been down, but I got up again, and I want other folks to know they can too. We all go through trials and tribulations but we have to bounce back from them. You don't just go through it, grow through it and never give up point blank period!! Suicide is never the answer.

Illness.

Connor Taylor-Parton

www.giftuksupport.org (GIFT) is the charity for Gastroparesis and Intestinal Failure. There is a supporters page at facebook.com/groups/GIFTuk

Almost three years ago, my 15-year-old sister Chloe fell ill; an illness that took a toll on her life physically and mentally. It started on the 21st April 2015. Chloe was supposed to be going to school that day, but she woke with feelings of nausea and dizziness, so Mum decided that she should stay at home. Soon after, Chloe tried to return to school, but her symptoms were too severe for her to cope, resulting in her repeatedly being sent home.

From the beginning, numerous people pushed their theories of what was wrong with Chloe onto our family. "It's all in her head" or "it's just a phase' were common responses, which only worsened Chloe's mental state as she desperately wanted to get better but didn't know how.

Her nausea made her unable to eat enough to sustain a toddler, let alone a teenage girl. Agonising pain sometimes flared up, resulting in countless trips to the hospital and doctors' appointments, yet her diagnosis was still undetermined. Having tried medical doctors, seeing a therapist for her mental distress was the next option, but it was evident from the first session that it wasn't going to work.

"When the doctors sort out your medical problems, the psychological problems will go away." The therapist said, "your depression is from you being tired of being ill," implying this was not a psychological condition. An eating disorder specialist and a counsellor both came to the same conclusion.

Another doctor asked Chloe if any of her friends suffered from the same 'illness', essentially accusing her of having an eating disorder and disregarding her physical suffering. The individuals who were meant to be helping Chloe were not believing her. Understandably this diminished any faith she had in them. Constant tests are mentally and physically draining for her. Even with a team of doctors and nurses searching for a diagnosis, nothing obvious has come up. With her GP and some other doctors still not having changed their mind about it being a psychological issue, Chloe often feels that they don't take her seriously. This is enough to make anyone feel desperately alone and anxious about being judged, which only worsens her depression.

She has lost contact with most of her friends since leaving school and has missed all the milestones for a girl her age: her sixteenth birthday, prom, festivals, concerts, house parties, first relationship – the list goes on. When friends do get in contact, there's not much to update them on.

Recently, her illness has taken a turn for the worse and Chloe can no longer leave her bed or walk by herself. Her only outings - to the hospital - are taken in a wheelchair, and she is fed through a tube to make sure she gets enough nutrients. Her mum sits by her bedside every night, reading forums and posts about other people in similar situations in the hope of finding a diagnosis. What started as a physical illness has progressed into an exasperating mental illness, too.

The percentage of patients who present to GPs with medically unexplained symptoms.
Stone, L. (2013)

25

Scarlet Evans

Asperger's.

Harry Reynolds

Autism support websites
www.autism.org.uk
www.childautism.org.uk

I was diagnosed at age four with Asperger's, though some diagnoses can happen sooner or later, depending on different factors. When I finally came out of my shell during sixth form, I was very upfront about my Asperger's, and it helped others to understand my behaviour and issues with aspects of my autism. They learned to understand it better and accept me for the person I am.

Being diagnosed with autism, or thinking you have it, is never as straightforward as labelling yourself with one defining set of characteristics and traits. There are around 700,000 people who have been diagnosed in the UK, more than one in 100. The terminology of the autistic spectrum is defined by the NHS as "the name for a range of similar conditions, including Asperger Syndrome, that affects a person's social interaction, communication, interests and behaviour".

The most commonly recognised distinctions with autistic individuals comes down to how we communicate with the world around us. Social skills that come naturally such as non-verbal behaviours like eye contact, expressing emotions, body language and gestures can be more difficult to engage with. It can take more time to adjust and learn these behavioural skills and there's no set time or certainty that you'll ever perfect them. For example, I still have difficulty maintaining eye contact, though interestingly I find this trait to be common with people in general. There's no shame in struggling to interact with others. You just need to try and work at your own pace.

When it comes to communication, maintaining conversation can be hard, but sometimes if a topic you enjoy discussing comes up it can make talking easier. I often find myself listening more than talking in discussions, unless I have something to contribute, but others can find themselves saying inappropriate things or being blunt. These scenarios can result in hurt feelings. Bluntness is a trait I find myself exhibiting a lot, and I tend to go straight to the point where others like to talk continuously. I learned to control what I said by listening to how others spoke to each other and reading the mood of a conversation.

One-on-one conversations can be very different, especially when romance is involved. In general, there'll be times of silence between people spending time with each other, but for some on the spectrum, a lack of conversation can lead to anxious thoughts, like "Am I boring them?" "Is this awkward?" From experience, I find that it's best not to make the long pauses seem awkward. Take time to think of things to say because even just being a good listener can lead to deepening relationships.

Often people on the spectrum are diagnosed at a young age. However if you feel that you are struggling, see a doctor about being diagnosed. It allows you and your condition to be recognised and opens up opportunities to be helped and supported. It also helps friends and family to understand and support you. I was fortunate, and I feel that anyone on the spectrum deserves to feel comfortable in their skin.

FED UP
OF LABELS

1

In every hundred people in the UK has Asperger's.
The National Autistic Society

Tourette's.

Marcus Brown

Tourette's support websites
www.touretteshero.com
www.tourettes-action.org.uk

Having Tourette Syndrome can create its fair share of awkward exchanges and confused looks, particularly accidentally winking at the passenger opposite you on public transport. It's an inherited neurological condition, the key features of which are tics, involuntary and uncontrollable sounds and movements.

Young people can be less understanding about mental health problems. This is often because of a lack of maturity or knowledge about the subject. When you're in school the condition can feel overwhelming and cause problems socially. As someone who has gone through school, I found the best way to deal with these attitudes is to approach the condition head on.

Coming to terms with the fact that you have a syndrome or mental health condition of any kind can be daunting. Many people, myself included, choose to try and ignore or reject their symptoms and hide them from other people. Whilst suppressing twitches can be an effective way of managing Tourette's, it's important not to be embarrassed or ashamed to have the condition. Explaining the condition to other people can help build an awareness around Tourette Syndrome and can sometimes lead to new friendships.

A question I'm often asked is, "Why do you do it?" or "What does it feel like?" An easy way to make people understand is to say that "it starts like a sneeze and the urge to release this sneeze or energy grows the longer it's left".

There is still a great deal of misunderstanding around Tourette's. Lots of people believe the misconception that all people with the condition have vocal or swearing tics.

A survey of undergraduates by University of San Diego psychologists Annette Taylor and Patricia Kowalski found that 65 per cent of people believed that everyone with Tourette's swears uncontrollably.

Tourette's with swearing is a condition known as coprolalia that in actual fact only affects between 10 and 15 per cent of people with Tourette's. Speaking to people about your condition can be one of the best ways to change people's perceptions.

Simple breathing techniques and taking time out of your day for relaxation can help to manage your symptoms as they often increase with stress. Tourette's can often differ at different points in your life - going through changes such as puberty, for example, you might notice it improving or becoming more noticeable. If your symptoms affect your daily life, it's important to talk to a doctor.

One of the important things to remember is that Tourette's is a not a limitation, you are still able to live a normal, successful life with the condition. Many celebrities have come out saying they have Tourette's including David Beckham and Russell Howard. In an age of social media, the growing awareness of all syndromes and mental health is only going to increase. Having conversations about these subjects will help to change people's minds.

0.3

The percentage of young people
aged 6 – 17 who have Tourette Syndrome.
Stern, Burza & Robertson (2005)

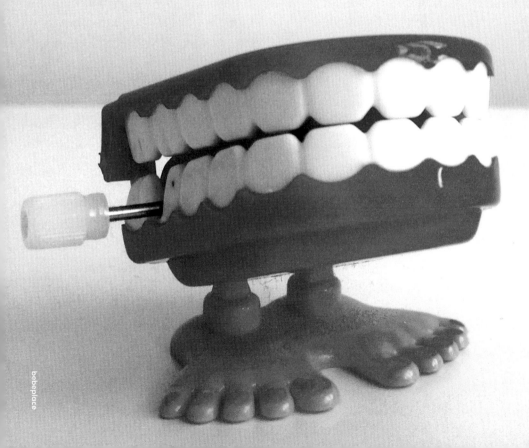

Katie Jordan

4.1

The percentage of people aged 16 to 24
who identify as lesbian, gay or bisexual.
Office for National Statistics (ONS) 2017

LGBTQ+.

Daisy Dalgleish

What have you learnt in sex-ed? What a healthy relationship is, how to have sex safely and the inner workings of your body? What you haven't learnt perhaps is how to remain safe in a homosexual relationship, how to understand your body as a transsexual and how those who identify as LGBT can remain healthy both physically and mentally.

Figures from the charity Stonewall show that only one in five LGBT pupils have been taught about safe sex within same-sex relationships at school. Their 2017 School Report also shows that 45 per cent of LGBT pupils reported being bullied at school.

James is a 20-year-old art student who identifies as LGBT. While in secondary school he struggled with his sexual identity and felt unequipped to form safe and healthy relationships. The failure to mention LGBT issues within sex-ed led to confusion and isolation. His experience of sex-ed consisted of himself and his 160 peers filling the school hall. The projector clicked, picture after picture of genitalia were blown up onto a giant screen, the hall was silent as the school science teacher lectured the congregation of 16-year-old boys about the dangers of sex.

The formality was almost painful, the hour consisted of heterosexual issues and information about heterosexual relationships. This was a lecture and not a lesson, not somewhere that James felt he could put his hand up to ask a question. Perhaps this sounds familiar?

James says: "I never learnt about my sexuality through school. I learnt Latin but I didn't learn about anything to do with my own identity, what that means and what to do with a guy. I turned to the internet, I read books. It wasn't until I went to art school that I really learned about myself.

"I learnt what two guys do through porn." This of course is problematic. James explains: "It creates an image of what you expect a gay relationship to be. Of course this is unrealistic, porn isn't real and it is dangerous to base the expectations for a relationship on it."

This is sadly the case at most schools within the UK. But equality campaigners are calling on the Government to include LGBT sex and relationships in its forthcoming new sex education guidance for schools. This would mean James and others like him can receive information and guidance within the safety of a school environment, without the dangers of looking for information through unregulated sources on the internet or forming relationship ideals based on porn.

If you feel that you identify with James's experience or maybe you know a peer who does, the resources on the sex ed, sexuality and gender pages in this handbook can help. You can also access these resources and call the helplines from within the MeeTwo app.

Josie Chiswell Jones

2,016

The number of youth referrals to gender
identity clinics in the UK in 2017
The Tavistock and Portman NHS Foundation Trust

Coming Out.

Charlotte

It took a great deal of courage for my son to come out as transgender. The school counsellor sort of helped him do so by calling me, though he was not actually fully ready to speak. She felt the urgency of the situation and the danger of not disclosing it. When we think about it, we believe that this call actually saved his life. He reckons that he would no longer be here if he had not talked about his trans-identity at that time.

I am so grateful he did. And I'm grateful he managed to face so bravely my first reaction.

The first 48 hours were a walk through hell. I'm a very tolerant and open-minded person, but still I completely over-reacted. I screamed, I cried, I went out for a long walk to sweat all my emotions and my fears out, leaving him alone with the feeling he had disappointed me.

But he had not. I was not disappointed; I was scared. And I was upset, distressed. How hard is it to hear your child say how much he hates himself, his name, his life, his body, when you are the one who gave him this name, this body and this life?

It's absolutely terrifying! Even more when you did not see it coming, when you thought everything was going fine. On top of that I had to fight the stereotypes and bias about trans-identity / transsexuality which were coming up to my mind, intensifying my fears. I could not see a future to this story.

It took me time to process what was actually my very own issues. And my son, courageously and patiently, gave me this time. Eventually I got all my emotions sorted and was ready to give him all the help he was begging for.

I had no reason, nor any right to deny him this help. With a new name, new pronouns, new look, he was still the same child I love so much. And when I look back at the daughter I've had, I do see the son I have today. He learnt to look back too, without anger.

Three years have passed now. He is followed psychologically and medically. After two years on puberty blockers he has finally started his real transition, his "real birth" with the testosterone injections. We should soon have his name officially changed and we are now planning his top surgery. It feels good to see him happier and at peace with himself.

I'm so proud of him, proud of us for choosing so rightly to follow together this difficult path, but oh so enlightening! It is the most incredible and prodigiously meaningful experience of my life. Thanks to my son, I've managed to tame all fears and I really know what love means. now .

Exam Stress.

Lily Wilson

Extreme levels of stress in the run-up to and throughout exam season affect thousands upon thousands of us annually. And what's worse is the age at which we're being affected is lowering rapidly. In the run-up to GCSEs last year, my mental health took a back seat; something I later realised I couldn't afford to allow. Prioritising work over anything else meant I was neglecting the much-needed rationalisation of the crazy thoughts which spin around my head daily. Ten days before the first exam I was threatened with inpatient treatment if I failed to turn things around; you know that feeling when everything suddenly becomes very real, and very terrifying? Well, yep, this was that moment.

I am in recovery from anorexia nervosa. An illness which almost took my life. An illness closely linked with anxiety. An illness which affects 1.25 million people in the UK alone. An illness which will manipulate, lie and isolate. An illness which is not glamorous or sexy or chosen. Why is this relevant? Well, since relapsing last year I've worked my ass off (and ironically, yes, I now have an ass – whoop to weight gain!) to get to a healthier place both physically and mentally. But watching the current year 11s and 13s go through the same stressful process I went through filled me with fear; fear for their current and future health.

I felt I had to do something so I wrote to, and later met with, our local MP to raise the issue of students' anxiety levels in the education system and highlight the detrimental effects the current system is having on our mental health.

We concluded that the current education system is failing us – if it weren't then we wouldn't have rising numbers of hospital admissions and CAMHS (Child and Adolescent Mental Health Services,) patients.

Meeting our MP to discuss the matter was incredibly valuable as it enabled me to gain understanding and different perspectives on the issue, two very positive things; however, I also learned one particularly horrifying truth: seven-year-olds are throwing up during exams due to anxiety. Seven-year-olds. Sorry, let me repeat that. SEVEN. YEAR. OLDS. Since when was this okay?

I came away absolutely horrified by this fact and as a result, have started a petition called 'Adapt the education system: lower student exam anxiety whilst saving NHS funds'. In order to get this serious issue up for debate in Parliament we need 100,000 signatures. I'm going to gather that by the fact you've read this far; you are, to a degree, interested in the subject. So now it's your turn to make a stand. Please support us in helping prevent both mental and physical illness in the future generations by signing the petition and sharing it directly to 10 people and asking them to do the same to enable us to create a ripple effect and increase signatures exponentially. We can make this necessary change. We can and we will. PLEASE SIGN AND SHARE!

Google 'Adapt the education system: lower student exam anxiety whilst saving NHS funds.' Or just scan the QR code at the top of the page

43

The percentage of suicides by people under the age of 20 related to academic pressure between 2014 and 2015. Almost one in three had exams at the time, or were waiting for results.

Suicide by children and young people in England - The University of Manchester, 2016

Ruby Evans

Revision.

Kyle Arthur

Revision is probably one of the worst parts about exam season. It takes time, it can be stressful, and all those books can sometimes seem overwhelming. These things considered, walking the dog or finally doing all your chores may seem like a better option than sitting down and getting to it. Even so, revision is a crucial part of exam success, whether we like it or not.

The first step to upping your revision game is to make a plan, a great reason to put those sharpies to use. "A timetable helps you to make sure that you know what's needed each day," says Ryan Smith, an English teacher at Mangotsfield School in Bristol. On top of helping you keep track of work, a revision timetable can also be a good way to create a healthy work/life balance, which is crucial for keeping the stress at bay. With a revision timetable, you'll know when you need to start revising and have a set goal to work towards. This goal might be a certain number of topics to cover or a time limit.

Once you've made a revision timetable it's important that you stick to it. Sticking to your plan will mean you get the right amount of revision done for each subject and also help develop discipline, a character trait that will help you in the world of work even after your exams are finished.

This might be stressful, but this can be a positive thing. It shows you're clearly consciously and actively doing things that will help you achieve," according to Smith. "That's the biggest mental hurdle and you've already jumped it!"

Don't revise too much. Yes, you read that right – don't spend too much time revising. This may seem counterproductive but cramming in your revision can be almost as bad as doing none at all. "You're better off doing short bursts, 20 minutes or so in the evening and a more extended time on the weekend," says Smith.

Ditch the distractions. Procrastination is a revision killer and it affects us all from time to time. The key tip for beating procrastination is to ditch your distractions. Smith recommends finding a space that becomes your 'work' place. Even as an adult, he admits finding procrastination difficult sometimes. "I either do my work at school or sit in the 'office' at home to do it," he says. "The temptation to procrastinate becomes far less."

Getting support from your parents, guardian, or even your friends can also help you stop procrastinating. This could mean telling your friends about your allotted revision times so they don't distract you on the phone or in other ways.

Reap the benefits. This is by far the best part of revision… when it's over! After creating a schedule, staying focused and being as disciplined as possible, you should feel confident going into the exam hall.

Directory

MEE
TWO

Support

Beat
The UK's Eating Disorder Charity

Access support via phone, email and one-to-one webchat with specially trained Helpline Advisors and online peer support groups and message boards. The BEAT website has lots of information about eating disorders. People always think of anorexia but eating disorders include bulimia and binge eating disorder too. Other conditions like emotional overeating, night eating and orthorexia (pure or clean eating) can cause significant emotional distress too.

Visit beateatingdisorders.org.uk

BEAT Youth Helpline: 0808 801 0711

*Open 12-8pm Monday to Friday
4-8pm Saturday and Sunday*

Men Get Eating Disorders Too
Run by men, for men

Advice, information and peer support website and chatroom for men with eating disorders.

Nice Guidelines
Know more than your doctor
Nice Guidance NG69 - google

A bit dry but it basically outlines the clinical guidelines for diagnosis and treatment of eating disorders.

Seed Eating Disorder Support

Hull based support group and drop in centre.

Telephone: 01482 718130

9.30am to 6pm weekdays

Self-Help

Dove Self-Esteem Project
There is more to Dove than soap

Dove developed these self-esteem resources for youth groups, but hey, you can download them too.

Be Real Campaign
Know you are not the only one

Jam-packed with personal stories, videos, advice and information, this is a fantastic resource. The campaign was formed in response to the Reflections on Body Image report from the All-Party Parliamentary Group on Body Image.

Body Gossip
Reimagine your relationship with your body

Write you own 'Body Story' on the Body Gossip website and share it with others.

Apps

Diet Or Disorder
Screening and self help tool

This is a free evidence-based app which has been created through a collaboration between the NHS and Swansea University with advice from the Child and Adolescent Mental Health Service (CAHMS), public health, education and primary healthcare professionals. Could do with some jazzing up, but it includes a simple screening tool, psychoeducation, self-help strategies, hints and tips for how to successfully seek help in primary care plus a single page format for presenting concerns to primary care professionals.

Good Blocks
Improve your self-esteem and learn to reject negative thoughts

A free app designed to improve your mood, your self-esteem and your body image. It helps you train your mind to reject negative thoughts in a fun and creative way. Available for IOS and Android. Some in-app purchases.

Rise Up + Recover
CBT Tool to monitor eating, record data and aid recovery

Using CBT (cognitive behavioural therapy) tools, this App helps you monitor your eating and the data you record can be exported as PDFs so you can store them or show them to your doctor. Available for IOS and Android.

Books

The Angry Chef
Bad Science and the Truth About Healthy Eating

Anthony Warner tears a chunk off the clean eating movement and then smothers it with butter and jam. Exposes the lies, pretensions and utter stupidity that pollute the world of food.

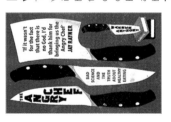

The Beauty Myth
Naomi Wolfs biting exposé of the nastiness of the beauty industry

Explores the tyranny of the beauty industry through the ages and its oppressive function in the home, at work, in literature and the media and in relationships. Don't call yourself a feminist if you haven't read this book.

Big Girl: How I Gave Up Dieting and Got a Life
Kelsey Miller

After following crash diets, healthy diets and nutritionist-prescribed eating plans, the author reached rock bottom. Then she learned how to eat based on her body's instincts: this book documents that journey of self-discovery.

Activities

Be a guinea pig
With The Centre for Appearance Research

The Centre for Appearance Research (CAR) is the world's largest research group focusing on body image. If you have something about your body that bothers you such as a birthmark, scarring or anything that has affected or changed your appearance, you could take part in the YP Face IT study. CAR is a collaboration between UWE Bristol, the BBC and the European Union. The website hosts podcasts, videos and a number of specially commissioned films on body image made for BBC Learning.

The Centre For Appearance - google Research for Resources + YP Face It

Make a statement
If you feel strongly about it, put it on a T-shirt.

All you need are some fabric paints, stencil cards, a paint brush and a T-shirt. It doesn't have to be perfect. Nor do you.

Media

Alexa Meade
Alexa turns people into paintings
She literally covers them in paint.

Body image & the media
Pana Chanthabandith

How media exposure impacts body image.

BBC My Mind & Me
Films and activities

An entire advice section all about Body Image, providing tips, videos and activities to help you feel better about your body.

Life Is Sweet
Directed by Mike Leigh

Brilliant 1990s British comedy-drama film and one of the first onscreen portrayals of teenage bulimia.

Super Size Me
Morgan Spurlock

For 30 days in 2003, Spurlock ate only McDonald's food. The film documents the drastic impact on his physical and psychological well-being, and explores how the fast food industry puts profit before health.

Life's too short to weigh your cornflakes
Anorexia as an identity

Catherine Pawley's ted talk about controlling food as a way of trying to minimise risk in an unstable world.

Support

NHS 111 Helpline
For any urgent medical concern
Call the NHS helpline on 111.
In an emergency always call or text 999.

NHS Choices
General information and advice
NHS Choices is an online service that provides a full A to Z of health information and services.

Youthhealthtalk.org
Personal physical and mental health stories.
Information, advice, videos and and strategies for teens who are living with physical and mental illness.

Doc Ready
Worried about seeing the doctor?
Doc ready takes you through the entire process step by simple step.

Young Men's Health
It makes us mad that when it comes to wellbeing, boys are completely ignored
Produced by the Division of Adolescent and Young Adult Medicine at Boston Children's Hospital, this website provides carefully researched health information specifically for young men. It is brilliant.

Self-Help

Teen Breathe
The only wellbeing magazine for teenagers
Revolutionary!
Packed with engaging and informative articles, the bi-monthly magazine is here to help you discover who you are, and offers tips, ideas and activities designed to encourage you to aim high and dream big.

Agnesforgirls.com
A life guide for teenage girls
Sensible, practical advice on everything from taking care of your mind to changing the world.

Apps

NHS Go
The NHS has an app!
NHS Go is a mobile version of NHS Choices but you can search for local services and it has dedicated health guides for teenage girls and boys.

Couch to 5k
A 3 times a week programme gets you running 5k in 9 weeks
You can be coached by celebrities Jo Whiley, Sarah Millican, Sanjeev Kohli or Michael Johnson. Excellent.

Down Dog
Yogaaaaah
Yoga strengthens the body, sharpens the mind, elevates your mood, boosts energy and improves sleep. Just do it.

Stepfinder
Finds the closest services to your current location
Homeless? Need contraception? Want mental health support? Stepfinder app uses GPS to help you find help you need. On iOS.

Kitchen Stories
Cooking from scratch is the only way to know what's in food you eat.
Easy recipes and cooking guides help you to learn how to cook in no time at all.

Books

Bad Science
Fun with pseudoscience

Ben Goldacre takes us on an eye-opening journey through the cynical exploitative world of Big Pharma.

This Is going To Hurt
Adam Kay

The often hilarious, at times horrifying and occasionally heartbreaking diaries of a former junior doctor, and the story of why he decided to hang up his stethoscope.

Mad Girl
Bryony Gordon

A bestselling biography about life with a mental illness. Ever since she was a teenager Bryony has felt that that her world is about to come crashing down: that her family might die if she doesn't repeat a phrase 5 times, or that she might have murdered someone and forgotten about it. It's caused alopecia, bulimia, and drug dependency. And Bryony is sick of it.

Activities

The Duke Of Edinburgh Award
Pick your challenge and raise money for charity

Choose from hundreds of activities – from canoeing to gymnastics, DJing to dog walking for an elderly neighbour – so there'll never be a dull moment. Plus, you'll pick up memories, friendships and skills that will stay with you forever. And the added bonus? Having a DofE Award can really give you the edge when you're applying for jobs, college or university. This is your chance to push yourself out of your comfort zone and do something that makes you, and everyone else, proud of you.

Dance Near You
Hip hop, Salsa, or Streetdance? Find the nearest classes on the dance near you website

Dancing is great for your physical and mental health. It makes you fitter, stronger, less anxious and improves self-esteem.

Media

Choice, happiness and spaghetti sauce
Malcolm Gladwell's TED Talk

Gladwell's TED talk shows how looking for perfection can often prevent us making the right choices and ultimately being happy.

Hackschooling
Logan LaPlante

After realising that all any kid warts to be when they grow up is happy, 13 year old Logan came up with a vision of what schooling should look like, with a strong emphasis on exercise, nutrition and relationships.

Bear's Grylls' mission with Anthony Joshua
Find this on YouTube

Anthony Joshua is a former Olympic silver medallist and current global heavyweight champion of the world. This fascinating episode will prove that even the fittest amongst us need to find the courage and motivation to overcome challenges.

This monk will change your world view
Jay Shetty on You Tube

Bullied as a child for being overweight, Jay lost two of his best friends, one in a car accident and one to gang violence. He spiralled out of control until at 22, he became a monk.

Support

The Sleep Council

How to get a good night's sleep

Sleep is fundamental to physical and mental health and wellbeing. The Sleep Council website provides helpful advice and tips on how to improve sleep quality and create the perfect sleep environment.

SleepHelp
From The Sleep Help Institute

People who don't sleep well are more likely to be depressed and anxious, and to be unable to process emotions the way they usually do. SleepHelp explains why sleep is so important.

Tired Out
The Teen Sleep Research Project

From keeping a sleep diary to the impact of diet and how sleep affects memory, 'Tired Out', which is part of the ongoing Teen Sleep Research project, has masses interesting facts, advice and research on the big ZZZZZ.

Self-Help

Nodcasts
100 Sleep Stories

Calm have created a fantastic selection of Sleep Stories and Sleep Music, which you can access on their website or through the Calm app. From Bob Ross, to Jerome Flynn from Game of Thrones, the stories have been listened to over 63 million times. Start with "Blue Gold," narrated by the actor Stephen Fry. His soothing voice wanders through Provence in the South of France, enjoying the smell of the lavender fields.

Darkness
Revolutionary, we know

If you can invest in blackout blinds, do. If not, wear an eye mask. Ear plugs are also useful because they block out distractions.

Temperature control

If you feel too hot or too cold, you won't sleep soundly. A cool temperature of around 16-18° C (60-65° F) is considered ideal.

Herbal teas

Camomile, lavender or passionflower can also help you relax.

Lavender oil

Sprinkling a few drops of lavender oil on your pillow at night will really help you sleep.

Apps

Relax Melodies
Sleep soundscapes

Achieve great sleep thanks to Relax Melodies, which allows you to create your very own sleepy soundscapes. Pick from over 100 soothing sounds and melodies, add a guided meditation specially made for sleep and drift into sweet slumber.

Night Shift Mode
Filter out the blue light that interferes with sleep patterns

The night shift setting on your phone changes the screen colour temperature so it is less stimulating

Pillow Automatic Sleep Tracker App
Get more ZZZZ's

Pillow is the best free sleep tracking app for your Apple Watch, iPhone or iPad with a unique set of features aiming to improve your sleep quality, help you wake up easier and fall asleep faster.

Moment
Put down your phone and get back to your life

If you're noticing that you're spending too much time on your phone, it's making you feel low or you want to reduce your phone usage then download the Moment app.

Books

Why We Sleep
The new science of sleep and dreams
Matthew Walker

A top sleep scientist argues that sleep is more important for our health than diet or exercise.

The Sleep Revolution
Arianna Huffington

The woman who set up the Huffington Post newspaper has turned her attention to sleep. In this book she explores the latest science on sleep and dreaming, takes on the sleeping pill industry, and explains why and how tech addiction is disrupting everyone's sleep.

Blame My Brain
The amazing teenage brain revealed.
Nicola Morgan

Nicola Morgan's carefully researched, accessible and humorous examination of the ups and downs of the teenage brain, including the need for more sleep, the urge to take risks, and the difference between the genders.

Activities

Take a warm bath
To cool yourself down

Soaking in warm (not hot) bath helps you get to sleep because it ends up cooling you down, especially as you dry off and the residual water on your skin evaporates. Adding essential oils such as lavender or Valerian turns bathing into aromatherapy.

The 4-7-8 Method
Dr Andrew Weil

The "4-7-8" breathing technique helps you fall asleep by increasing the amount of oxygen in your blood stream, slowing your heart rate, and releasing more carbon dioxide from the lungs.

Instructions:
- Place the tip of your tongue against the ridge of tissue just behind your upper front teeth.
- Exhale completely through your mouth, making a whoosh sound.
- Close your mouth and inhale quietly through your nose to a mental count of four.
- Hold your breath for a count of seven.
- Exhale completely through your mouth, making a whoosh sound to a count of eight.
- Repeat the cycle three more times for a total of four breaths.
- ZZZZZ

Media

Why school should start later for teens
Wendy Troxel - TedX

Teens don't get enough sleep, and it's not because of Snapchat, social lives or hormones -- it's because of public policy, says Wendy Troxel. Drawing from her experience as a sleep researcher; clinician and mother of a teenager; Troxel discusses how early school start times deprive adolescents of sleep during the time of their lives when they need it most.

Why do we sleep?
Russell Foster -TED

When you're asleep, your brain doesn't shut down. In fact, some areas of the brain are actually more active during the sleep state than during the wake state. Russell Foster explains how our perception of light influences our sleep-wake rhythms.

David Attenborough
Sleep with a national treasure

A study conducted by scientists in the UK, New Zealand, and the Netherlands has found that watching nature documentaries has the same positive effect as meditation on feelings of wellbeing. Watch Blue Planet and Planet Earth episodes on YouTube.

Support

The Student Room
Peer support from GCSE onwards
Students supporting each other - we salute peer support. From GCSEs to University, this site provides advice, info, practice exam papers, revision resources, and online support services.

Not Going To Uni
There are other things you can do!
This website is a treasure trove of alternative career and training options.

Osborne Cawkwell
Tutoring that builds confidence by integrating positive psychology
Specialising in the introduction of private tutors by the hour in London, and online and residentially in the UK. Their mission is to ensure the tutors on their books are clued up on the mental health problems young people face. Daniel Licence is their mental health adviser liaising with tutors, clients and other related specialists.

My Tutor
One-to-one tuition via skype
The tutors are handpicked from across the UK and just one in seven applicants is selected. It's expensive, costing between £18 and £36 an hour, but MyTutor students see their results increase by an average of +1.7 grades.

mytutor

Self-Help

ChildLine
Beat Exam Stress Guide
A great free download of dos and dont's and useful tips to help make things better.

Martial Arts Clubs UK
Kick back at exam stress
Martial arts teaches focus, builds patience, and helps young people deal with pressure. This free directory lists all the martial arts clubs and schools providing Judo or karate in the UK

Apps

BBC Bitesize Revison
Videos, tests, info, the lot
Take the stress out of revision with Auntie Beeb

Duolingo
If you are learning a language you need this app.
Any time, anywhere bitesized chunks of language learning in your pocket.

Gojimo
Revision app
Access over 40,000 free questions and track your progress.

Quizlet
Search millions of study sets or create your own.
Study with flashcards, games and more.

Crossword
Improve your word power and exercise your brain.
Over 750 free crosswords in an app

Plant Nanny
Better grades in an app
Plant nanny is a game that reminds you to drink water and water your plants. It's important not to get dehydrated, especially when you are trying to revise because not drinking enough can cause headaches and make you feeling dizzy, moody and tired.

Books

Ideas Man
Sheridan 'Shed' Simove lives and breathes ideas.
Every day of his life dozens of new ideas spring from his astonishingly active mind. And if an idea hasn't been done before, then Shed is sure to attempt it.

Fighting Invisible Tigers
Stress Management for Teens
Earl Hipp's guide to managing stress in all situations, including exams, with this activity book, filled with real life stories and interesting facts.

Activities

Pomodoro
The #1 study timing technique
Pomodoro is one of the most widely used timed productivity methods in the world. You can use an alarm clock or your mobile if you don't have your own pomodoro timer.

How Pomodoro Works:
1. Choose a task to be completed.
2. Set the timer to 25 minutes.
3. Work on the task until the timer rings.
4. Take a short five minute break.
5. Every 4 Pomodoros take a longer break of up to half an hour.

Canva
Free mind map maker
Organize your thoughts, plan your revision, brainstorm, take notes or work through complex problems by making beautiful visual representations of problems and solutions.

Woodcraft Folk
Outdoor learning and world piece
Woodcraft Folk is an educational movement which aims to boost young people's resilience and increase awareness. Every week thousands of volunteers and young people all over the UK meet in the community to learn about big ideas through fun activities like singing, camping, playing and debating.

Media

I don't give a damn about your degree
Elon Musk - YouTube
Bill Gates didn't graduate from college. Nor did Steve Jobs. But you'd still hire them. Musk believes the current education system doesn't allow students to achieve their full potential, so he set up his own school with no grading levels for his five kids! Musk seems to have gone a bit bonkers recently but there is no denying his genius.

My year of saying yes to everything
Shonda Rhimes - TED Talk
Shonda Rhimes describes how she got her mojo back by saying yes to everything.

5 Keys to Break Through Stress
Tony Robbins (Legend) - YouTube
The difference between a great performance and poor performance is not intelligence or ability; most often it's the state that your mind and body is in.

Inside the mind of a master procrastinator
Tim Urban - TED Talk
Funny and thoughtful insight into procrastinators, which will leave you feeling light-hearted, but also motivated to stop the cycle of procrastination.

Support

The Prince's Trust
Training and employment support

Set up to transform the lives of 11 to 30-year-olds who are struggling at school (Idris Elba went through their programme). They run special programmes to help you build confidence and achieve your true potential. The website explains how they can help you get into training and employment. If you're thinking of a career in STEM check out how fashion retailer ASOS uses them. Call them to find out more.

Freephone: 0800 842 842
Or text 'Call Me' to 07983 385 418
Monday to Sunday, 9.00am to 9.00pm

Citizens Advice
Help with benefits, housing, legal advice and much more

Citizens Advice can help you to resolve all sorts of practical issues by providing free, independent and confidential advice. They have a specific section for young people aged under 18. You can use their web chat online or call their national advice line.

England: 03444 111 444
Wales: 03444 77 20 20

Coram Children's Legal Centre
Experts in young people's rights

They provide legal advice and/or representation for protection, education, immigration and juvenile justice.
Contact: 01206 714 660

Self-Help

Why Comics?
A cool way to be better informed about what is going on in the world

Why Comics? explores contemporary humanitarian and social issues such as racism, conflict, migration, trafficking and climate change through interactive comic books based on real-life testimony. Its a great way of learning. In fact researchers at Sheffield Hallam University have found that comics are a better educational resource than traditional textbooks!

Talk Like TED
The nine public speaking secrets of the world's top minds

Nervous about speaking or just want to feel more confident conversing with others? This book will show you how to focus on what you want to say and communicate it clearly

Reprezent
Tune in to youth led radio: 107.3 FM

Reprezent is a radio station that is run by young people for an audience aged between 13 and 25 across London.

Apps

Naturespace
Relax more and sleep better

Immerse yourself in holographic sounds from the natural world. We live in a world that strongly emphasises vision, yet we rely on sound to tell us about our environment and to gauge whether we are safe or not. We listen, both consciously and subconsciously, to the everyday sonic landscape to determine the safety of our surroundings. By supplying your brain with extremely realistic, tranquil natural environments, free from the auditory chaos of urban life, your mental state responds with relaxation. Naturespace is an effective, drug-free solution for combating stress and anxiety, aiding sleep and relaxation, and enhancing focus and concentration

Habit Bull
Break bad habits

Not all habits are bad, but there are some that need changing if they are affecting your health. This free app allows you to break bad habits or build positive ones.

Art Guide
Be more creative

This free app by Art Fund is an on-the-go guide to discovering great art across the UK. You will be able to discover over 700 museums and galleries plus all the best exhibitions across the UK. Art Fund also have a National Pass which gives you discounts or free entry to loads of places in the UK.

Books

Slay In Your Lane:
The Black Girl Bible
Yomi Adegoke and Elizabeth Uviebinené

The long-awaited, inspirational guide to life for a generation of black British women inspired to make lemonade out of lemons, and find success in every area of their lives. From education to work to dating, this inspirational, honest and provocative book recognises and celebrates the strides black women have already made, while providing practical advice for those who want to do the same and forge a better, visible future.

Freakonomics
Assume nothing. Question everything.
Steven D. Levitt & Stephen J. Dubner

What is cheating and why do people cheat? What is the most effective way to reduce crime? These are just some of the questions that this book answers, but you should know:

Be More Pirate
Sam Conniff Allende

Allende draws parallels between the strategy and innovation of pirate legends with modern day rebels, like Elon Musk, Malala and Blockchain, and reveals how to apply their tactics to life and work today. Be More Pirate will show you how to leave your mark on the 21st century. It's also a bloody good read.

Activities

UK Youth Parliament
Be part of the Make Your Mark scheme to select the topics that the UK Youth Parliament debate in the commons. The UK Youth Parliament provides opportunities for 11-18 year olds to use their elected voice to bring about social change through meaningful representation and campaigning. Go online and get involved.

Groundwork Youth
Now is the time to go green

Groundwork Youth is a platform supporting 16 – 24 year olds to take action in their local environment. They provide opportunities and experiences to develop leadership and connect you with people who also want to make a difference in their communities. Sign up to their bulletin to find out about future activities and youth programmes.

GROUNDWORK

CHANGING PLACES
CHANGING **LIVES**

Volunteering
Brilliant for your sense of self and a great way to gain experience and build your CV

It is difficult for teenagers to get paid employment but lots of places will be happy to let you help for free. Try and volunteer in an area that you are interested in. For example, if you like animals, see if you can help out at a local farm or animal shelter. Like ponies? Offer to sweep the yard and clean the horses in exchange for the odd lesson.

Media

Hip Hop & Shakespeare?
The awesome Akala - TEDX

"To destroy the beauty from which one came!", Akala asks the audience whether this quote is Shakespeare or hip hop? The audience answers Shakespeare. He tells them it's from a gentleman called Shawn Carter, also known as Jay-Z. In this talk, Akala demonstrates and explores the connections between Shakespeare and Hip-Hop and the wider cultural debate around language and it's power. Brilliant

A teen scientist's invention to help wounds heal
Anushka Naiknaware - TEDX

Working out of her garage, Anushka Naiknaware designed a sensor that tracks wound healing, making her the youngest winner (at age 13) of the Google Science Fair. Her clever invention addresses the global challenge of chronic wounds, which don't heal properly. Anushka's creative 'smart bandage' is embedded with tiny monitors that allow medical workers to 'see' whether a dressing needs changing without disturbing the wound.

How to live before you die
Life lessons from Steve Jobs in a speech at Stanford University - TED

Steve Jobs was adopted, he never graduated and he was fired from Apple. He was also a genius.

Support

Ditch the Label
Research, advice and useful information on bullying

Support for young people who are being bullied or are struggling with mental health, body image, sexuality and hate crimes.

DITCH THE LABEL YOUR WORLD. PREJUDICE FREE.

National Bullying Helpline
Provides support for parents and teenagers

Helpline : 0845 22 55 787

Monday to Friday, 9am to 5pm

Lots of practical information plus downloadable booklets on the website too.

Bullying UK
Advice and information

Part of the Family Lives website which is largely for adults, but the bullying chat forum is good.

Bullybusters
Liverpool, Sefton and Knowsley

Helpline: 08001696928

Regional charity funded to provide support to Merseyside, excluding Wirral.

Self-Help

Bullying: What Can I Do?
Respect Me Scotland

Scotland's anti-bullying service has created several really helpful video campaigns around bullying. The What Can I Do? YouTube video contains really practical advice on all the different things you can do if you are being bullied.

Storybooth
Record your story and let the Storybooth team turn it into an animation

This is our new favourite thing. DO IT!

Discover Your Secret Powers
The only person who missed more school than Keri Smith had cancer.

But the author of Wreck This Journal had a secret power. She had ideas. Check out Keri Smith's website for loads of inspiration and self-help advice.

From the Post Carbon Institute by Keri Smith (c) 2014 by permission of the author

Apps

ForMe
The ChildLine App

Childline is well known as the UK's biggest children's helpline, but they actually support young people up to the age of 19. In 2017 they launched ForMe, an app where you can get advice and support on a huge range of issues including friendship, peer pressure and bullying. You can also call a ChildLine counsellor or login to 1-2-1 chat from within the app.

MeetUp
Do new things. Meet real people

Meetup brings together groups of like minded people with a shared interest all over the world. The Youth section is not huge but the fantastic thing about MeetUp is you can start your own group. From Art Groupies to Zipwire Zombies, you simply pick a MeetUp name, describe the age range of the people you want to meet, then set up your first event in a public location and wait for people to sign up.

HelloTalk
Make friends and learn to speak their language

A really clever app that connects you to people of a similar age in different countries so that you can practise your language skills while making a new friend at the same time. It's free to use for a single language, but you pay if you want to converse in more than one. As if.

Books

Queen Bees & Wannabes

Helping your daughter survive cliques, gossip, boyfriends, and other realities of adolescence,

You may not have heard of Rosalind Wiseman, but the film 'Mean Girls' (2004) is based on her New York Times bestselling book about the complexities of teenage friendships. If you read one book...

Bullies, Cyberbullies and Frenemies

What do Kate Middleton, Lady Gaga and Christiano Ronaldo have in common?

Yup, they were all bullied. Michele Elliot's book explains what bullying is and all the different disguises it uses to make you feel inadequate.

Activities

Drama classes

Find your inner thespian!

Taking drama classes can increase your self confidence and create empathy. But it can also be fun and help you develop your communication skills.

National Citizen Service

For 15 to 17 years olds

NCS is a 3-4 week experience that helps build your confidence and self belief so that you can take on anything in life. Live away from home, develop life skills and make friends. Food, accommodation and activities are included for just £50. Bursaries available.

Call: 0800 197 8010

Teen Talk in a jar

Emotional health in a jar

Discussions, starting points and icebreakers on just about everything teenagers want to talk about. Helps you kick off great conversations with friends or parents.

Media

Wonder

How to be different

A film based on the bestselling story by RJ Palacio (2012) about a boy with facial differences who enters a mainstream school.

To this day, for the bullied and beautiful
Shane Koyczan

It's hard to stand up for yourself if you don't know who you are. Poet Shane Koyczan delivers his hilarious and thought-provoking take on what it's like to be young, different and a bully...

Mean Girls
Seriously...

If you haven't seen this film you have missed an important cultural and developmental milestone. Get the popcorn, grab the remote and watch Rachel McAdam and 'The Plastics' define mean. Undoubtedly Lindsay Lohan's finest hour.

Support

Domestic abuse
Women's Aid and Refuge
Support for all victims of domestic abuse, their friends and family, including coercive control, emotional, sexual and physical violence. Call the Free 24 Hour National Domestic Violence Helpline.
Women's helpline: 0808 2000 247

Victim support
For victims of crime
A UK charity offering support for victims of crime, their families and also witnesses of crime.
Victim Support line: 0808 1689 111
Open 24/7, 365 days a year

Happy Steps
Support for stepfamilies
The UK's only research based stepfamily resource centre. Advice and support for stepfamilies along with couple workshops and coaching.

Forced Marriage Unit
Forced marriage is illegal in the UK
No one, even a parent, has the right to force you.
Helpline: 0207 008 0151 Mon-Fri: 9am to 5pm
Out of Hours: 0207 008 1500

Riprap
If You Have A Parent With Cancer
Run by a specialist cancer nurse with a chat forum where you can post and get support from other young people.

Self-Help

Keep a journal
Create family memories by documenting your family in words and images
It can be easy to forget the good times when things are not going well, so keeping an ongoing journal where you document family events in words, photos and drawings can be a helpful reminder that it is not always difficult.

Talk to yourself
Got something awks to say? Practice saying it out loud in front of the mirror.
Rehearsing the tough stuff makes you feel more confident when you finally pluck up the courage to throw it down.

Teen Issues
Read, learn and share your story
The Family Life section of this website offers advice and information on everything from strict parents to family conflict. You can share your story and get support at the bottom of each article.

Apps

WhatsApp
Create a whatsApp family group
Call it something fun like 'Masters Of The Semi' or 'Smith Street Massive'. Make it the go-to place for all the family to share info. If you live between two parents its a great way to keep everyone in the loop. Screen shot the funnies, print them and stick them in your family journal (see left).

Stay safe
Share your location via GPS
Tracker apps mark your location so your family can always find you.
Find My Friends Apple
Life 360

Remember The Milk
Free to-do app
Families work better when everyone pulls their weight so creating a shared to-do list with push notifications is a good way to spread the load and avoid arguments.

Books

Fun Home
Alison Bechdel
Literally the best comic novel about family, secrets and sexuality that you will ever read. It took seven years to produce because Bechdel photographs herself in poses for each human figure before drawing!

Let's Pretend This Never Happened
Jenny Lawson
Jenny recalls her eccentric childhood.

Dress Your Family In Corduroy And Denim
David Sedaris
Sedaris is just brilliant on the extraordinary quirks of his family.

Activities

Family meals
The family that dines together, whines together... less
Psychological research confirms that you are less likely to grow up crazy and/or stupid if you eat dinner with your family on a regular basis. If you actually cook the dinner, your chance of pocket money increases significantly.

Family outings
Life beyond the living room
Doing things together helps strengthen family bonds and they don't have to cost money. River swimming, hiking, climbing, picnics, visiting museums and galleries are free for all. Even if you only manage one outing a month, you are building family memories.

Family games
Old-fashioned but still fun
Cluedo, Monopoly, Scrabble, Poker, Charades: games are a great way to bring out everyone's inner child and spark a little healthy competition.

Cleanathon
Make cleaning competitive
Get everyone, including parents, to agree to spend an hour cleaning the house together with a cash prize for the person who works the hardest.

Media

Little Miss Sunshine
Anti-establishment family satire
The Hoover family's hilarious road trip to get seven-year-old Olive to a beauty pageant in California.

The Kids Are All Right
Starring Julianne Moore with Annette Benning and Mark Ruffalo
One of the first mainstream movies to show a same-sex couple raising two teenagers. A smart, warm and moving statement on family values.

Boyhood
Directed by Richard Linklater
Filmed over 12 years with the same cast, Richard Linklater's Boyhood is a ground breaking story of growing up as seen through the eyes of a boy named Mason who literally grows up on screen before our eyes. Absolutely brilliant.

Mrs Doubtfire
Directed by Chris Columbus
Hilarious classic which broaches the serious subject of post divorce barriers to child access.

Parenthood
Directed by Ron Howard
The funniest, most moving, most well observed film about family life.

Support

Child Bereavement UK

Support for people who have lost someone they love

Grief is normal no matter who it is that you have lost and talking about it helps.

Helpline: 0800 028 8840

Email: support@childbereavementuk.org

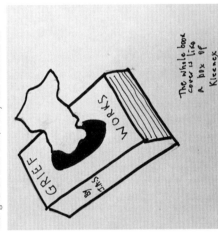

Child Bereavement UK
REBUILDING LIVES TOGETHER

Hope Again

Website for young people living with loss

A Cruse Bereavement website offering information, a listening ear and advice for any young person dealing with the loss of a loved one.

Helpline: 0808 808 1677

Monday to Friday: 930am to 5pm

Email: hopeagain@cruse.org.uk

Help 2 Make Sense

Support for grieving young people

Really nice website with friendly resources on everything from ways to remember to advice on how to help a grieving friend. They have a confidential ASK email service where you can get free and confidential support as well as getting specific or practical questions answered.

Email: ask@winstonswish.org

Self-Help

Men and Grief

Huffpost Blog

Rick Belden believes that male grief is all too often invisible, misunderstood, and unwanted, which leaves many men in the difficult position of having to deal with grief on their own, if they deal with it at all.

The whole book cover is like a box of Kleenex

Grief Works

Julia Samuel MBE, psychotherapist

Julia Samuel MBE, is a psychotherapist who specialises in grief, who worked to launch and establish Child Bereavement UK. Her website, Grief Works is based on a book she wrote by the same name. On the website, you can access the 8 Pillars of Strength to help you work through grief.

Apps

Grief

For 11-25 year olds who have experienced bereavement

Created by a group of young people who have lost someone, this app contains stories, films and information about grief. It also includes a built-in notepad so you can write down your feelings. In-app links allow you to access support organisations near you through the Child Bereavement UK website.

Smiles & Tears

Friendly bereavement app

Designed by Norfolk based child bereavement charity Nelson's Journey, this app was designed for younger children, but when you have lost someone you love, it feels comforting to be treated like a child. The app allows you to record memories, send virtual gifts and write thoughts, feelings and emotions. It also provides tips on how to manage emotions such as anger, confusion, guilt and loneliness. The app is available for download on Android and IPhone.

Books

Healing Your Grieving Heart for Teens
Dr Alan Wolfelt

This book contains 100 practical ideas to help you to understand, express and cope better with your grief.

Sad Book
Michael Rosen

Michael Rosen is one of Britain's favourite and most successful authors. This book is about his grief at the death of his son Eddie from meningitis at the age of 19. Sincere and simple, it acknowledges that sadness is not always avoidable, or reasonable, and it helps readers understand very complicated feelings.

A Monster Calls
Patrick Ness

Raw, emotional and cathartic, A Monster Calls is a novel that deals with grief, loss, and anger through the most compelling storyline. This book won Patrick Ness the Carnegie medal for children's writing in 2012 and it has now been made into a film.

Activities

Young People's Advisory Group
For young people aged 11-25

Run by Child Bereavement UK, YPAG is an opportunity for bereaved young people to get together and meet others who have also experienced the death of someone important in their life.

The groups meet regularly to work on projects to create resources that will help other bereaved young people. Sessions are free to attend. You just need to have access to transport. The groups take place after school, between October and May and are currently running in Milton Keynes, Newham (East London), Runcorn (Cheshire) and Saunderton (Buckinghamshire).

Plant a flower, a tree or even a whole garden
A beautiful way to remember a loved one

Planting something beautiful is a lovely way to honour their memory and it also creates something for you to look forward to in the future.

Media

Mad World
Prince Harry

In this podcast, Prince Harry speaks to the Telegraph's Bryony Gordon about his mental health experiences. The conversation provides listeners with a candid insight into the innermost thoughts of a modern young royal who lost his mother, Princess Diana, and the effect it had on him.

Extremely Loud and Incredibly Close
A young boy's search for meaning after his father dies in the 9/11 catastrophe

A movie about catastrophic loss, and a special child who is somewhere on the autistic spectrum, trying to make sense of something that literally doesn't make sense to him.

The Descendants
A film about loss, grief and betrayal

This film examines the complicated feelings that occur after the death of someone whose behaviour denies those left behind the opportunity to idealise them.

Captain Fantastic
Explores how death is different for everyone

Ben, his wife Leslie and their six children live deep in the woods of Washington state, isolated from society. When Leslie dies suddenly, Ben must take his kids into the outside world for the first time.

Support

Talk to Frank
Drug and alcohol support

If you need emergency help, or are worried about a friend or relative's drug use.

Helpline: 0300 123 6600. Text: 82111
Open 24 hours a day, 365 days a year.

Alateen
Support for young people (12-17) whaffected by someone else's drinking

For information of local Alateen meetings, please email them at enquiries@al-anonuk.org.uk.

Helpline 0207 403 0888
10 am - 10 pm, 365 days a year.

Addiction Helper
Advice on treatment

Free, confidential NHS or private help for anyone who is affected by drug & alcohol addiction.

Helpline: 0800 44 88 688
Free 24/7 365 days a year

Hope for children of Alcoholics

Self-Help

Young Addaction
1-2-1 support plus local outreach work in schools

As well as one-to-one work and group support, Young Addaction offer a range of early intervention programmes in schools, youth clubs and other youth friendly settings.

Re-Solv
Working to end solvent abuse

Expert charity working to support those whose lives are affected by solvents, gases and other 'legal' highs. If you misuse any of these products, or if someone you know misuses them, call the helpline.

Helpline: 01785 810762
Text/Whatsapp: 07496 959930
Monday – Friday, 10am – 4pm

National Association for Children of Alcoholics

Information, advice and support for everyone affected by a parent's drinking, including adults.

Helpline: 0800 358 3456
Friday, Saturday and Monday: 12 to 7pm
Tuesday to Thursday, 12 to 9pm

Alcoholics Anonymous
Group meetings for over 16's

Twelve steps to sobriety with the help of peer support. Under 16's need to be accompanied by an adult.

Helpline: 0800 9177 650

Apps

Drink Aware
Alcohol tracking app

The free app from Drinkaware will help you to track your alcohol consumption, calculate units and calories and set goals to help you moderate your drinking. It also pinpoints locations where you need extra help and lets you set goals tailored to your existing drinking habits.

AA Big Book
The text of the AA bible in an app

The free AA App developed by Alcoholics Anonymous has it all, from personal stories to recovery podcasts and a sobriety calculator to manage how far you've come if you're drinking too much.

Quit That!
Habit Tracker App

This easy to use free app lets you track all of the stuff you are trying to quit, whether its drugs, alcohol or smoking.

Books

Drop
Katie Everson

Nominated for the 2016 Carnegie Medal. Drop does not sugar coat the reality of teenage drug use and pressure. This is an honest, non-judgemental, unbiased read that will inform, advise and reassure.

Recovery: Freedom from our Addictions
Russell Brand

We are all addicted to something and Russell Brand knows well having suffered from many addictions in the past. He also questions what it says about society today, in an age of consumerism

Activities

Wait a minute
Crush your cravings one minute at a time

When you next get a craving, make yourself wait one minute before you give in to it. The next day, make yourself wait two minutes. The day after, wait three minutes. Build up the time until eventually, you can ride it out completely.

Amy Winehouse Foundation
Drug & alcohol prevention programme for schools

The Amy Winehouse Foundation works to prevent the effects of drug and alcohol misuse on young people. The Amy Winehouse Foundation Resilience Programme is a drug & alcohol awareness and prevention programme for secondary schools. Trained and accredited volunteers use their own experiences of substance misuse and recovery to educate students, parents and teachers about the triggers for substance misuse and what can be done to prevent it.

The Program
Downloadable PDF of Russell Brand's reinterpretation of the AA's famous 12 step program

Brand has taken the fundamentals of the traditional abstinence model, left out the God bit and added in a few swear words. Mind you, there are still mantras and references to higher powers so it is not completely free from divine intervention.

Media

Girl, Interrupted
Winona Ryder and Angelina Jolie

This film tells the true story of Susanna Kaysen, an eighteen year-old girl who chases a bottle of Aspirin with a bottle of vodka, but denies that she was trying to kill herself. She is sent to a mental institution and diagnosed with "Borderline Personality Disorder." She makes friends with Lisa (Angelina Jolie), who plays a brilliantly convincing sociopath who controls relationships. You never quite find out whether Susanna tried to kill herself, but the film explores the thin line between sanity and madness.

Rose's experience of taking legal highs
BBC Teach

Legal Highs are not only dangerous, but have contributed to many deaths in young people in the UK. In this short film, Rose describes how taking a legal high at a festival nearly killed her. This courageous story shows the need for support, understanding and community.

Simply Complicated
Demi Lovato opens up

You may know her as a global superstar, but Demi has suffered from addiction, abuse and low self esteem. This video charts how hard she struggled to get launched as a singer and the demons that conspired to undo her success.

Support

CEOP
Child Sexual Exploitation and Online Protection Command
CEOP keep children young people safe from sexual abuse and grooming. If an adult has made you feel unsafe, scared or worried on or offline, report securely to CEOP using their online reporting button.
www.ceop.police.uk
They take all reports seriously and will do everything they can to keep you safe.

Cybersmile
Advice on cyberbullying
Helpful website featuring topics ranging from Netiquette to Doxing - someone sharing your personal information online.

True Vision: Report It
A website to report online hate crime
In the UK it is an offence to stir up hatred on the grounds of race religion, disability, gender or sexuality.

Internet Watch Foundation
Practical assistance in reporting and removing content online
Childline and the Internet Watch Foundation (IWF) work together to help support individuals under 18 with removing intimate content online. You can make a report online via the IWF Website.

Self-Help

Thinkuknow
Relationships and the internet
Thinkuknow is the education programme from CEOP. Visit Thinkuknow for advice on the possible risks you may face online and how to respond as safely as possible – they also offer advice if you're worried about a friend. Advice for parents and careers and resources for professionals such as films and lesson plans for use with children and young people aged 4 – 18.

UK Safer Internet Centre
Stay safe on social media
Online safety tips, advice and resources to help children and young people stay safe online.

Get Safe Online
Free expert advice website
Information on identity protection, gaming, clickjacking, apps, cyberbullying and much more.

Childnet
Advice on all aspects of internet safety
The Childnet website is for 11 to 18 year olds and provides top tips, blogs, competitions, resources and advice on internet safety.

Disrespect Nobody
Healthy and unhealthy relationships
Information on sexting, consent, porn, relationship abuse, rape and harassment, the law, negative consequences and practical advice.

Apps

Zipit
Nip unwanted chat in the bud
If someone is sexually harassing you or asking you to send them naked selfies, the free Zipit app by Childline lets you respond with a smart GIF put down. The app also contains tips on on how to be safe during intimate chats and you can call Childline from within the app too.

Bright Sky
Free app supporting people in abusive relationships
The 'My Journal' tool allows you to record incidents of abuse via text, audio, video or photo form, without any of the content being saved on the device itself. This app also includes information about online safety, stalking, harassment and sexual consent.

Super Better
Turning life's challenges into a game
A clinical trial funded by the National Institute of Health and conducted at Ohio State University Wexner Medical Center and Cincinnati Children's Hospital found that using SuperBetter improves mood, decreases anxiety and suffering, and strengthens family relationships. Apparently.

Books

Everybody Lies
What the internet can tell us about who we really are. Seth Stephens-Davidowitz

This book shows how big data can give us surprising new answers to important and interesting questions. One of his main arguments is that people lie when they present their "ideal selves" on social media but they tell the truth when they are typing into search engines. Makes sense.

Selfie: How the West Became Self-Obsessed
Will Storr

Selfie takes us from the shores of Ancient Greece, through the Christian Middle Ages, to the self-esteem evangelists of 1980s California, the rise of narcissism and the selfie generation, and right up to now, our very own era of hyper-individualistic neoliberalism. Stop the world. We want to get off.

Shamed
Jon Ronson

Ronson spent three years travelling the world meeting recipients of high-profile public shaming. This is a book about the cruelty of social media and shaming.

Activities

The Bullying Workbook for Teens
Activities to help you deal with social aggression & cyberbullying

Raychelle Lohmann wants you to know that anyone can be bullied, whether you are popular in school or a straight A student. This book will provide you with anti-bullying tips and strategies that will guide you on a journey to confidence and hope.

Upstand! Be the hero
Don't be a bystander

Being a bystander to bullying is like saying you agree with the bully which is so not cool. An upstander is someone who stands ups and takes action in defence of others to stop the bullying. If you see someone being bullied online, or it's happening to a friend, the Upstand website can help you do the right thing.

Play The Digizen Game
A Childnet Website

In the game you have the opportunity to experience a day at school with Joe, the main character, and make decisions about how to help him as he experiences cyberbullying. You are challenged to be a responsible digital citizen but it also teaches you more about keeping safe online.

Media

Cyberbully
Starring Maisie Williams

Maisie Williams, or 'Arya' to Game of Thrones fans, plays a teenager who is in a race against time to stop a cyber stalker. This docu-drama reveals not only how some bullies don't realise the effect their words or actions have on others, but also how threats of social isolation can change a person's thoughts and emotions.

Your Online Life, Permanent As A Tatoo
Juan Enriquez- TED Talk

Bloody terrifying. In this short talk, Juan Enriquez looks at the permanent effects o² digital sharing on our personal privacy. He shares insight from the ancient Greeks to help us deal with our new "digital tattoos."

#StopSpeakSupport
Campaign from the Royal Foundation which is aimed at 11-16 year olds. YouTube

Animated guide explaining what you need to do if you spot bullying online. The clue is in the title

Early 1990's Internet Commercial
It's way before your time but... google it

Back in the time before big data ate all the kittens, people actually had to sell the idea of the internet as a useful addition to the household.

Support

Teenage relationship abuse
Advice from the Ava Digital Prevention platform

Explains all the different types of abuse including coercive control as well as the legal issues.

#LoveDontFeelBad
A guide to healthy behaviour in intimate relationships

Videos, quizzes, mythbusting, advice and info on what to expect and what not to tolerate in a romantic relationship.
Developed by Women's Aid.

Adolescent Romantic Relationships: Headspace
Downloadable PDF from the Australian National Youth Mental Health Foundation

Adolescents typically have little or no prior experience of developing romantic relationships. Inexperience also means young people cannot rely on the benefit of past experience when trying to problem-solve relationship difficulties or gain perspective on them. This can be particularly problematic when it comes to coping with break-ups.

Your Thoughts on Falling In Love
TeenHealth Survey

Results of a survey of more than 5,700 teenagers who took a survey on what it feels like to be in love.

Self-Help

Brook: Enduring Love?
Survey Findings on couple Relationships in the 21st Century

The Enduring Love project was conducted by the Open University and Brook, The Sexual Health Charity. Brook present a selection of the most important findings from the study on their website. You will find lots of helpful information from the study on topics such as cheating, intimacy, trust and jealousy, relationship myths and more.

WikiHow
How to Date Successfully...

As a Teenage Girl
As a Teenage Guy

Apps

Mend
Break up self care app

Daily audio bites, mending exercises, progress tracking and personal stories to help you get over heartbreak. The app is free for the first seven days so aim to mend your broken heart in a week.

Youper
An app to help people with shyness and social anxiety gain more confidence in social situations.

They use neuroscience, design, and technology to help users develop social skills which can be useful for dating, making the first step to speak to someone you like or communicating in a relationship.

Nearify
View a list of local events and invite friends who might be interested.

You can also sync it with your Facebook profile to see what events your friends are attending — so, you know, you can just happen to show up at that concert your crush is attending!

Books

Dating & Sex: A Guide for the 21st Century Teen Boy
Andrew M Smiler

Written for younger teenage boys, this book addresses common questions about what's typical, and provides a framework for sex, puberty, and healthy relationships. Helps boys identify what feels right for them in a variety of common situations.

The First Time
True tales of virginity lost and found

Kate Monro's groundbreaking and very personal insight into modern sexuality. Men and women, old and young, gay, straight, Christian and Muslim talk about losing their V card.

The Guide:
Managing douchebags, recruiting wingmen, and attracting who you want. Rosalind Wiseman

How do you get out of the friendzone (where girls refuse to take you seriously)? What's the right way to react when getting made fun of?

How do you talk to your parents so that they'll actually listen? With the help of hundreds of high school aged boys, Rosalind has identified and answered the most pressing questions teenage boys have.

SURVIVAL VOL 1

THE GUIDE

MANAGING DOUCHEBAGS, RECRUITING WINGMEN, AND ATTRACTING WHO YOU WANT

ROSALIND WISEMAN
WITH ASSISTANCE FROM HIGH SCHOOL GUYS AROUND THE COUNTRY

Activities

Dating
Duh, obviously

The great thing about social media is that it connects you to huge networks of people, but you are still more likely to meet someone if you look locally. School is the obvious place to start, but youth clubs, sports centres, shopping malls or the park are also good options. Remember the bigger your social network the better, so don't rule anyone out. That geek your mum keeps trying to introduce you to? She may not be the one but hey, have you seen her best friend?

Movie Night
No date? No problem

Grab your popcorn and your best buddy and work your way through our definitive guide to teenage relationship movies.

The Breakfast Club (1985)
Heathers (1988)
Clueless (1995)
Romeo + Juliet (1996)
10 Things I Hate About You (1999)
Almost Famous (2000)
Love Actually (2003)
Juno (2007)
Angus, Thongs and Perfect Snogging (2008)
Twilight (2008)
Moonrise Kingdom (2012)
The Perks of Being a Wallflower (2012)
Sing Street (2016)
Call Me By Your Name (2017)

Media

Why You Will Marry The Wrong Person
Alain de Botton

The philosopher questions whether the western idea of romance has ruined our relationships and explores how we can manage expectations in a relationship?

How to Fix a Broken Heart
Guy Winch - TED talk

At some point almost every one of us will have our heart broken. Based on his book of the same name, Guy Winch explores the science behind why we keep going down one rabbit hole after another, even when we know it's going to make us feel worse.

40 Days of Dating
Jessica Walsh and Timothy Goodman

Fantastically self-indulgent experiment tracking two single friends who decide to date each other for 40 days.

Friends
Never gets old

The most streamed TV show on Netflix despite being 25 years old, Friends still has much to teach us about the complexities of relationships.

Support

Brook

Free, confidential online and clinic based sexual health service for young people under 25
Brook have sexual health clinics all over the UK and their 'Find A Service' facility will direct you to your nearest Brook clinic or appropriate alternatives. Whether you need contraception, abortion referrals or sexual assault services, Brook can help. They also offer a 24/7 online Ask Brook information service.

The National Sexual Health Helpline

Free helpline provided by Public Health England
For advice and information on sexual health.
Helpline: 0300 123 7123
Monday to Friday, 9am to 8pm.

Rape Crisis

For the victims of rape, sexual assault, child sexual abuse or any form of sexual violence
Helpline: 0808 802 9999
Monday to Sunday, 12pm-2.30pm and 7-9.30pm
Operates 365 days a year.

Free Contraception

We love the NHS
Contraception is free on the NHS from Brook, GPs, pharmacies and clinics. Condoms or femidoms protect against the transmission of STIs while the implant provides protection against pregnancy for three years. Use 'em all!

Self-Help

Sexwise

Advice on sex, contraception, pregnancy, STIs and pleasure
Led by the the Family Planning Association (FPA), the Sexwise website can answer questions and help you find free contraception, STI testing and treatment.

Morning after pill

It is definitely not good to use the morning after pill as a form of contraception but...
It can be used to prevent pregnancy up to five days after having unprotected sex. Levonelle and ellaOne are free from Brook/family planning/sexual health clinics, some pharmacies and most walk in clinics. It costs around £30 to buy. Only ellaOne can be sold to under 16s without a prescription.

HPV Vaccine

If you can get it, take it.
Girls in year 8 are offered two doses of the HPV vaccination to protect against cervical cancer (the most common cancer in young women). It is about to be offered to boys in the UK because there has been a dramatic increase in cancers in young men. Until that is rolled out, GP's and pharmacies may offer to vaccinate boys privately.

WUKA Period Pants

No more pads or tampons needed
The UK's first eco-friendly, reusable period underwear - leak-free, comfortable, soft against the skin, and easy to use. Stylish and secure, these are a game changer.

Apps

Flo

Flo is way more than just a super-slick app to track your periods. Log in your mood and symptoms to see how they change and repeat throughout the cycle. Our favourite part is 'Insights' with tons of info on topics nobody talks about, like masturbation or pubic hair. Fun educational pieces about how your body works and what "that Latin word" actually means allow you to ask any question anonymously and get opinions from all over the world.

My Sex Doctor Lite
Sex and sexual health app

This is a free sex ed app featuring a sex dictionary and a 100 Things You Must Know list with topics ranging from puberty and menstruation to sexual orientation, safe sex, pregnancy, and contraceptives. The sex ed dictionary provides definitions on everything from from acne to abortion to acquaintance rape.

Sex Positive
Sexual Health Wheel Of Fortune
Created by the University of Oregon, this is basically a Wheel of Fortune for all your sexual health questions. You can "spin" a pair of wheels by choosing a body part (like your mouth) and another object or body part (someone else's mouth) to calculate the STI risks that come with the interaction. Advice from experts. Only on Android

Books

Sex: A Book for Teens:
An uncensored guide to your body, sex, and safety. Nikol Hasler

The funniest, punchiest straightforwardest book on sex ever written.

Girls & Sex – Navigating the Complicated New Landscape
Peggy Orenstein

Based on in-depth interviews with over seventy young women and a wide range of psychologists and academics, Peggy Orenstein pulls back the curtain on the hidden truths, hard lessons, and important possibilities of girls' sex lives in the modern world.

The Self-Esteem Team
Guide to Sex, Drugs and WTFs?!!
Grace Barrett, Natasha Devon and Nadia Mendoza with a foreword by Zoella.

Activities

Solo Sex
As Woody Allen said, "don't knock it, it's sex with someone you love."

Masturbation is literally the last taboo standing, but teenagers can learn a lot from self love. It comes more naturally to boys, but girls who masturbate understand the way their bodies work better than girls who don't. Masturbation is still a subject that doesn't get discussed, and there will be all sorts of eye rolling when the 'authorities' spot this tiny paragraph, but we don't care because masturbation is a fundamental part of sexual development. It feels great. Its safer than drugs and it doesn't get you pregnant, or expose you to sexually transmitted infections. What's not to like?

Jackinworld
Everything a boy needs to know, and then some
The world's most comprehensive website devoted to masturbation.

Media

Tea & Consent
Fantastic YouTube video which uses making a cup of tea as a metaphor for sexual consent

If they are unconscious, don't make them tea. Unconscious people don't want tea and can't answer the question "do you want tea?" because they are unconscious. Ok, maybe they were conscious when you asked them if they wanted tea, and they said "yes", but in the time it took you to boil that kettle, brew the tea and add the milk they are now unconscious. You should just put the tea down, make sure the unconscious person is safe, and – this is the important bit – don't make them drink the tea."

Hanah Witton
Sex Ed Vlogger
Straightforward advice and information on sex. Her '10 Masturbation Hacks' has had 1.2m views. Respect.

Sex etc.
SexEducation for teens, by teens
Website covering sex, relationships, pregnancy, STIs, birth control, sexual orientation and much more.

Scarleteen
The way sex education should be
Supportive sex education resource which has been written and designed specifically for young people.

Support

LGBT Foundation
Advice, support and helpline
Working to ensure LGBT voices are heard and their needs are met.
Helpline: 0345 330 30 30
Monday to Friday from 10am to 6pm
Saturday times may vary.
Email: info@lgbt.foundation

Switchboard
Advice, support and helpline
Talk with trained volunteers who identify as lesbian, gay, bisexual or trans. Nothing is off limits and everything is confidential.
Helpline: 0300 330 0630 Every day 10am to 10pm

Terrence Higgins Trust
Advice and information
Lists out of hours sexual health clinics in your area.
Helpline: 0808 802 1221
Monday to Friday, 10am to 8pm
Email: info@tht.org.uk

Albert Kennedy Trust
Need help with housing, employment, training and education?
The Albert Kennedy Trust exists to help young people aged 16 to 25 who identify as LGBT find safe homes and employment.
Helpline 020 7831 6562 Mon - Fri, 10am to 4:30pm

Self-Help

RUComingout
Thinking about coming out?
The RUComingout website contains over 300 real life stories about coming out written by people from all over the world. It also includes exclusive interviews with authors, actors and other public figures who wanted to share their experiences of coming out.

Just Like Us
Work with schools to raise awareness and decrease stigma. Celebrate difference by encouraging your school to take part in their Diversity Week.

The Proud Trust
Find your nearest LGBT group
Search using your post code to find your nearest youth group and connect to other young people just like you.

LGBT Youth in Care
Know your rights
Provides downloadable resources about rights and support for LGBT people in care.

Imaan
Supporting LGBTQ Muslims
Imaan was founded in 1999 in London to help families and friends to address issues of sexual orientation within Islam.
Contact: info@imaan.org.uk

Apps

Distinc.tt LGBT+
The first social networking app for LGBT+ people aged 12 and over
Currently only available on IOS and by all accounts, it's a bit buggy but it is a brave move to create an app that helps young LGBT people to connect. Unlike the MeeTwo app it is neither anonymous, nor moderated in advance, so be careful.

LongStory
LGBTQ+ friendly dating sim app
Set in 'Weasel Heights' Middle School. Pick your avatar, your pronouns and who, if any, of your friends you want to date. First three episodes are free.

Huddle
Video sharing mental health app linking young LGBT people.
If you are not comfortable identifying yourself you can pixelate your video and create a pseudonym. There is, no voice augmentation, so someone could still possibly decipher your voice. Unlike the MeeTwo app it is neither anonymous, nor moderated in advance, so be careful.

Books

Oranges Are Not The Only Fruit
Jeanette Winterson
Coming to terms with her unorthodox sexuality in a strict Pentecostal household in the industrial Midlands.

Dykes to Watch Out For
Alison Bechdel
Acerbic cartoons about 1980's lesbian culture.

Boy Meets Boy
David Levithan
A love story between, yep, you guessed it.

Call Me By Your Name
André Aciman
Beautiful book. Beautiful film.

Tales of the City
Armistead Maupin
First published in 1978, this series was the first positive portrayal of gay, lesbian and trans relationships to mainstream audiences.

An Outsider Inside
RJ Samuel
Irish-Indian lesbian activist, Jaya's survival depends on hiding the truth of who she is and who she loves – from herself.

an outsider inside
R J Samuel

Activities

Stonewall Youth
Start your own Stonewall LGBT youth group
For support with coming out, gender identity, staying safe online and how to set up an LGBT group. Download their free Coming Out guide. There's also a lot of information on their main site and on Stonewall Youth.
Information Line: 08000 502020
Email info@stonewall.org.uk

Celebrate World Pride
Host an LGBT awareness day at your school
June 28th marks the anniversary of the Stonewall riots in New York which started the Gay Liberation movement. Celebrate by having a Pride day at your school. Create a special assembly, wear rainbow colours, invite guest speakers and throw a party.

Media

Nanette
Hannah Gadsby - Netflix
Australian lesbian comedian Hannah Gadsby recounts her experiences with homophobia and sexual assault, and broader themes of violence against women and male impunity. Funny, moving and insightful.

Love, Simon
We really do love Simon
Simon is in the closet but he finds the confidence to come out after corresponding with an anonymous friend online. Really tender affecting film.

Shh! Silence Helps Homophobia
LGBT Youth Scotland YouTube
Created by the Fife LGBT Youth group.

Born Julia and Julius
Animation on being born intersex - YouTube
Animation about the challenges of growing up intersex in Uganda.

Yoruba Richen
What the gay rights movement learned from the civil rights movement TED talk
A moving and insightful talk.

Jenni Chang & Lisa Dazols
What is LGBT life like around the world? - TED
Travelling to 15 countries to find brave LGBT people.

Support

Mermaids UK
Supporting gender diverse young people and their families

Mermaids UK have been supporting gender variant and transgender children, young people and their families since 1995. Whether you are feeling isolated or just need information and support, Mermaids are there to help.

Email: info@mermaids.org.uk
Helpline: 0344 334 0550
Monday to Friday, 9am to 9pm

The Beaumont Society
The largest and oldest support group for transgender people and ther families in the UK

The Beaumont Society operate a 24 hour helpline, 365 days a year where you can get anything from advice to just someone friendly to talk to.

Helpline: 01582 412220

Self-Help

The Good Men Project
A website which asks what it means to be a good man.

A website that explores masculinity, gender, sexuality and fatherhood from a liberal and usually well-informed perspective.

Everyday Sexism
A website which explores women's rights and gender equality

The Everyday Sexism Project exists to catalogue instances of sexism experienced on a day to day basis.

Gendered Intelligence
Knowledge is Power

Pronouns, passports, trans clothing exchanges, gender-neutral hairdressers are all listed in the Ka-Pow Resource page.

Gender Identity Clinic:
Tavistock & Portman NHS Foundation trust

Highly specialised clinic for young people experiencing difficulties with their gender identity. Based at the Tavistock Centre in north London with satellite units around the country, the waiting time for a first appointment is now at least 14 months. The website has lots of information and links to Channel 4's documentary series Kids on the Edge about young people and mental health. The first episode follows the stories of two trans children, Ash and Matt.

Telephone: 0208 938 7590

Apps

Final Fantasy IX
Gender fluid app from the final fantasy series, age 12+

Features Quina Quen, who is from a tribe of creatures called the Qu. Her/his pronoun depends on the language in which the game is played, and his/her appearance doesn't indicate a gender.

Christella VoiceUp
Voice-training coaching app

Only for MTF, Christella's app analyses your voice by gender and then coaches you to voice up.

Testo Memo
Testosterone injection reminder

Testosterone shots must be done on a regular basis. Testo memo calculates when your next shot is due and sends you a notification beforehand.

Gender Neutral Toilet Finder
It really is the small things...

The brainchild of a trans youth group in Newcastle upon Tyne, this app helps you locate the closest gender neutral toilet. It's a peer support project so the app relies on you to contribute new locations when you come across them. You can also rate gender neutral facilities for their accessibility, cleanliness and other features.

Books

Stone Butch Blues
Leslie Feinberg

One of the first novels to seriously explore the gender identity. Feinberg, who died in 2014, was "an anti-racist white, working-class, secular Jewish, transgender, lesbian, female, revolutionary communist." The book's protagonist Jess is equally fascinating. **transgenderwarrior.org**

Beyond Magenta
Transgender teens speak out. Susan Kuklin.

Six transgender teens tell their story to the author and photographer Susan Kuklin.

Trans Youth
Sexual Health Booklet

Somebody needs to call the design police, but aesthetics aside, this booklet does tackle all the really thorny issues head on.

Guide for young trans people in the UK
Downloadable booklet

Again, this looks like it was designed by an accountant. Actually, it's an NHS publication so there's a good chance it was. Super informative though.

Becoming Nicole
The transformation of an ordinary family

Amy Ellis Nutt spent almost four years with a traditional family who adopted twin boys, one of whom transitions from Wyatt to Nicole.

Activities

Join a trans youth group
Gendered Intelligence runs youth groups for young people who are trans, non-binary or questioning.

The groups are held in London, Leeds, Bristol and there is a partnership project in Hertfordshire. Young trans people aged 11 or over are welcome to attend the Under 16 group in London. The Leeds and Bristol groups are open to young people aged 13-20.

Get your hair cut at a trans friendly hairdressers
Open Barbers, London
Bookings: 07546 017849

Barberette, London
Bookings: 07522 873333

Halo Hair Salon, Cambridge
Bookings: 01223 837792

Simone Thomas, Bournemouth
Bookings: 01202 760003

Simone Thomas, Wokingham
Bookings: 01189 760003

Media

Fifty Shades Of Gay
Tillett Wright - TED talk

We are constantly putting labels on one another; 'gay', 'straight', 'bi' or 'trans'. But are we ever one thing? Artist and photographer Tillett Wright has a truly unique story to tell. Worth watching.

My Genderation
Trans themed videos by Fox, lewis and Owl

If you have ideas for films or interviews, they'd like to hear from you.

Lee Mokobe
"My mother said I could grow up to be anything. I decided to be a boy."

Lee Mokobe's powerful TED talk describes what it feels like to be transgender and explains how people continue to confuse gender and sexuality.

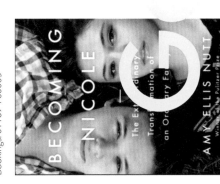

School

School-based counselling

School is the best place to look for support because you can either access counselling within the school or get a referral to CAMHS (see right). Read Emma Selby's interview on page B20 in the Expert section for a more complete explanation of how school counselling works with CAMHS.

School counsellors are one of the most widely available forms of psychological therapy for children and young people and provision is increasing. Talking to a counsellor offers you an opportunity to explore and understand your difficulties within a relationship of agreed confidentiality. On average, school-based counselling is approximately three to six sessions and young people say it can be very helpful. School counsellors don't have the same qualifications as mental health specialists, so if your problems are more severe they will refer you to the Child and Adolescent Mental Health Services (CAMHS) (See right).

School counselling is a NICE recommended intervention for mild depression and there is evidence to suggest that it is effective at reducing distress and helping young people achieve their personal goals. Targeted school-based interventions can also reduce school exclusion. The government plans to have specialist mental health teams in one in every four schools by 2022.

Doctor

Seeing a doctor without your parent's permission

Anyone can make an appointment to see a doctor, no matter how old they are.

If you are registered with a doctor and are under 16, you may be asked why you want to see the doctor alone but it is only to make sure you are safe. If you need treatment such as antidepressants they will probably advise you to tell your parents or an adult that you trust because you will need additional support. Everything that is said between you and the doctor is confidential. That confidentiality can be breached if you, or someone else is in danger, but your doctor will explain this to you in more detail.

Online GP Access

In some areas, once you are over 16 you can book doctor's appointments online

You can usually add a message to let the doctor or nurse know why you want to see them which can be helpful if you are shy, or if it is something that might be embarrassing to say over the phone.
Downloadable PDF: Young people's access to GP online services Patient Guide

Doc Ready

Website that prepares you before you talk to a doctor about your mental health

Doc Ready helps you to build a checklist for your appointment and gives advice such as knowing your rights and how to give feedback or make a complaint.

CAMHS

CAMHS

Child and Adolescent Mental Health Services. Read Emma Selby's interview on page B20 in the Expert section for a more complete explanation of how CAMHS works.

CAMHS are the NHS services that assess and treat young people with emotional, behavioural or mental health difficulties. CAMHS support covers depression, problems with food, self-harm, abuse, violence or anger, bipolar, schizophrenia and anxiety, to name a few. There are local NHS CAMHS services all around the UK, with teams made up of nurses, therapists, psychologists, support workers and social workers, as well as other professionals. You can refer yourself to CAMHS in some areas but nearly half (43.4%) of referrals to CAMHS come from schools or GP's. As more areas adopt single point of access numbers, self-referral will become easier.

As Emma Selby points out in her article, your best bet is to go through school as they know the right numbers to call. When you are referred to CAMHS, the CAMHS team then decide whether they think they will be able to provide useful support for your family. The threshold for treatment is high and there can be a wait between the time the referral is made and the first CAMHS appointment. You can find your nearest CAMHS service through NHS Choices website. The My CAMHS Choices website has information, videos and resources.

Therapies

Cognitive Behavioural Therapy
Helps you to change unhelpful ways of thinking and behaving

CBT takes a hands-on, practical approach to problem solving. Its goal is to change patterns of thinking or behavior and so change the way you feel about yourself. In adults, 50% of CBT patients make a full recovery. Read Lord Richard Layard's article on page B16 in the Experts section for more information.

Dialectical Behaviour Therapy
Helps you to change unhelpful behaviours, but also focuses on accepting who you are

The goal of DBT is to help you learn to manage your difficult emotions by letting yourself experience, recognise and accept them. Recommended for young people who have a history of self-harm and who have difficulty managing their emotions.

Family Therapy
The whole family works together with the therapist

This can help communication and allow the family to understand the impact of issues around children's behavioural problems, disability, family breakdown, addiction and domestic violence.

Psychotherapy
Longer-term therapy which involves talking about the effects of past events

Psychotherapy helps you to understand yourself through your relationship with your therapist. The one-to-one relationship interaction helps you to think about your personal difficulties in terms of how your feelings and thoughts are connected to your relationships and behaviour, and how past experiences can affect your current relationships.

Private Therapy
If you can afford it

The cost of talking therapy varies, but a one hour session can cost between £50 and £150 depending on where you live. It is essential to check that the therapist is listed on one of the registers of approved practitioners.

Approved therapist registers
- British Association for Counselling and Psychotherapy (BACP)
- Association of Child Psychotherapists
- British Psychological Society
- Youth Wellbeing Directory
- Association for Family Therapy (AFT)

Online Therapy

Silvercloud
Available via an NHS referral for young people over 16

Silvercloud uses cognitive behavioural therapy (CBT) to help you change the way you think and feel about things. Work through a series of topics chosen by your therapist at your own pace where and when it suits you. The therapist will check in with you about once every two weeks during the course to review progress. The course features videos, activities, quizzes, audio guides and your own online journal.

Welldoing
Find an adolescent therapist

This website is a portal to real world or online sessions with therapists who specialise in working with children and young people.

Be Mindful
Mindfulness-based cognitive therapy course

A web-based training programme that guides you through all the elements of mindfulness-based cognitive therapy. The course costs £30 for ten half hour sessions which consist of videos and interactive exercises led by leading mindfulness trainers. There are also guided meditation audio downloads, guides on how to practice mindfulness in your daily life and online tools to review your progress.

Support

Papyrus

Suicide prevention helpline for young people (under 35)

If you are at risk of suicide, or are worried about someone else being suicidal call the Hopeline and talk to a trained volunteer:

Hopeline: 0800 068 41 41

Text: 07786 209 697

Mon to Fr, 10am - 5pm and 7pm to 10pm

Weekends, 2pm to 5pm

PAPYRUS
prevention of young suicide

Samaritans

For under 18's as well as adults

Email jo@samaritans.org, or talk face to face in one of their 201 branches. You don't have to be suicidal to contact them. You can just talk.

UK & Ireland Helpline: 116 123 (UK)

Welsh Language: 0808 164 0123

Available 24/7, 365 days a year.

CALM

Male suicide prevention

Around 70% of youth suicide is male so The Campaign Against Living Miserably (CALM) is specifically aimed at men.

National helpline: 0800 58 58 58

London Helpline: 0808 802 58 58

5pm to Midnight, 365 days a year.

Self-Help

U Can Cope

A film made by The Samaritans

Compelling stories of surviving suicidal thoughts, with commentaries from leading clinician Dr Alys Cole-King and eminent academic Professor Stephen Platt. The film promotes three main messages:

1. **Anyone can have suicidal thoughts.**
2. **There is always hope.**
3. **There is always help.**

Zero Suicide Alliance

Everyone who reads this book should take the free 20 minute take this free online suicide prevention training course.

The course will enable you to identify when someone is presenting with suicidal thoughts/behaviour and show you how to support them and signpost them to the correct services.

Make a safety plan

Download a suicide safety plan from Papyrus

When thoughts of suicide are overwhelming, staying safe for even 5-10 minutes takes a great deal of strength. This plan is to use during those times; it isn't a plan of how to rid yourself of thoughts of suicide, it looks at staying safe right now so that you still have the chance to fight another day and access the support you need and deserve.

Apps

MY3

Who are the three people you would call if you felt suicidal?

Is it your brother? Your friend? Maybe even a neighbour down the street? Customise your safety plan by identifying your personal warning signs, coping strategies, distractions and personal networks. This safety plan will be with you at all times and can help you stay safe when you start thinking about suicide. Download MY3 to make sure that your three are there to help you when you need them most.

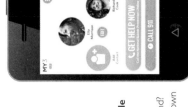

Stay Alive

Free suicide prevention app

This app is a pocket suicide prevention resource for the UK, packed full of useful information and tools to help you stay safe in crisis. You can use it if you are having thoughts of suicide or if you are concerned about someone else who may be considering suicide. Includes a Safety Plan to use if you have a crisis and need to keep yourself safe. You can upload photos that are important to you from your phone in the 'LifeBox', add your own crisis support phone numbers in 'Find Help Now', fill in your 'Reasons For Living' and add to a list of ideas for 'Taking Care of Yourself'.

#StayAlive

Books

Remember This When You're Sad
Maggy Van Eijk

Maggy knows where the best place to cry in public is: the top deck of a bus, right at the front. She also knows that eating super salty liquorice or swimming in an icy cold pond are things that make you feel alive but aren't bad for you. This book is about anxiety, depression, panic attacks, teenage bulimia and disassociation. But it's also about being a young woman with the added pressure of having an untrustworthy mind.

Your Illustrated Guide to Becoming One with the Universe
Yumi Sakugawa

We absolutely love this. Nine beautifully illustrated metaphysical lessons, including; how to slow down, appreciate your surroundings, overcome your insecurities and feel more connected with the world around you. Yumi also has an app YUMIVERSE on iOS. You might notice some of Yumi's work in this book!

Activities

100 Ways To Get Through the Next 5 Minutes
Ideas to change your mind

US charity, Life Line provides support for people living with suicidal thoughts and suicide attempts. From stargazing to adopting a pet insect, this website offers an extensive, sometimes fun, sometimes ridiculous list of things to do to distract yourself from feeling down.

Sing
Karaoke, Musically, Spotify, Choir?

Sometimes listening to loud music and singing ar the top of your lungs can help you feel better. Even if its just a little better, it's still better.

Learn your triggers
Keep a diary, a journal or a sketchbook handy

Most of the time we don't know why we feel low, but keeping a journal or tracking when we might know can be enlightening. When you start to feel hopeless, make a note of what is happening in your life at the time, it could be anything from exam deadlines to starting your period or feeling disconnected to eating too much cheese...

Media

ManTalk podcast
Jamie Day

A series of podcasts tackling issues surrounding men's mental health. Supported by the charity CALM.

Stranger On The Bridge
Jonny Benjamin

In 2008, twenty-year-old Jonny Benjamin (below right) stood on Waterloo Bridge, about to jump. A stranger saw this and stopped to talk with him – a decision that saved Jonny's life. The Stranger on the Bridge is a memoir of the journey Jonny made both personally, and publicly to not only find Mike - the person who saved his life (pictured left), but also to explore how he got to the bridge in the first place.

HeadTalks
Informs, inspires and engages those interested in mental wellbeing

Insightful videos and podcasts on a range of topics, from suicide to loneliness, depression to stress and much more.

97

Support

Self Harm UK

Dedicated to self-harm recovery and support.
Supports teenagers by giving them a safe space to talk and ask questions. Great resources on their website, including videos, articles, blogs and self-help guides.

Self Injury Support

Support for females of all ages
Free confidential Self Injury helpline plus resources on coping strategies etc.

Free Helpline: 0808 800 8088
Tuesday to Thursday evenings, 7 to 930pm.

Text Help: 07800 472908
Tuesday, Wednesday, Thursday, 7 to 9.30pm

Harmless

User led organisation
Online support, advice and information, coping strategies and ways to help yourself, or your friends.

SANE

National out-of-hours helpline
Sane offers specialist emotional support, guidance and information to anyone affected by mental illness, including family, friends and carers.

SANEline: 0300 304 7000
4.30pm to 10.30pm, daily

Self-Help

Self-harm.co.uk/Alumina

Free online self-harm programme
Run by SelfharmUK this confidential weekly chat room for young people aged 14+ is run by a team of trained counsellors.

THRIVE

Self-harm resource pack
Downloadable PDF with detailed info on self harm as well as a long list of alternative coping mechanisms.

Life Signs

Self-Injury Guidance & Support
Downloadable self-injury fact sheets. Check out the HALT technique and the advice section for males.

The Mix: What Men Need

Let's stop telling men to 'man up' and start telling them to open up
Join in this important discussion about men and mental health issues through The Mix website.

Apps

Calm Harm

Approved by the NHS to help you to ride out the urge to self harm
Calm Harm is an award-winning app developed for teenage mental health charity stem4 by Dr Nihara Krause, consultant clinical psychologist, using the basic principles of Dialectical Behavioural Therapy (DBT). Calm Harm provides tasks to help you resist or manage the urge to self-harm. You can make it private by setting a password, and personalise the app if you wish. You will be able to track your progress and notice change.

BlueIce

Prescribed app designed to be used with face to face care within the mental health service
Evidenced-based app to help young people manage their emotions and reduce urges to self-harm.

Developed with the Oxford Health NHS Foundation Trust and co-produced by young people who self harm. The app includes a mood diary, a toolbox of evidence-based techniques to reduce distress and it will automatically route you to an emergency number if the urge to self harm continues.

Books

A Bright Red Scream
Marilee Strong

Marilee Strong explores the hidden self-harm epidemic through case studies, research from psychologists, trauma experts, neuroscientists, and insights from self-harmers including troubled teenagers, middle-age professionals and grandparents. Strong explains why self-harm helps people manage overwhelming fear and anxiety, and explains how you can heal yourself and learn to break the self-destructive cycle.

Skin Game
Caroline Kettlewell

A memoir of Kettlewell's life as a self harmer. She began cutting at 12 as her body began to change and the cutting continued for another twenty years.

Mind Your Head
Juno Dawson with Dr Olivia Hewitt

Clinical psychologist Dr Olivia Hewitt with humorous reassurance from Dawson helps you understand a range of conditions from anxiety to personality disorders, as well as being straight-talking about body image, relationships, drugs and alcohol.

Activities

The Butterfly Project
Self harm coping technique

When you feel like you want to cut, draw a butterfly in that area. Name the butterfly after someone you love - Justin Bieber? Panic At The Disco? Meghan Markle? If you cut before the butterfly is gone, you've killed your beloved. If you don't cut, it lives. If you have more than one butterfly, cutting kills all of them. Another person can also draw them on you if you like. These ones are extra special, so take care of them. Even if you don't cut, you can draw one and name it after someone you know that self harms or is suffering and tell them. It could help.

Cut To Create
Instead of cutting yourself, cut up magazines and make a collage to express how you feel

Hate the way they use skinny models in fashion mags? Can't stand Donald Trump? Furious about the cost of university? Get scissors and glue and cut out relevant images, stick them together and paint or write your opinions over the top. Take a photo of the image, email it to us at art@meetwo.co.uk and we'll publish it in the MeeTwo app.

Bite into something disgusting
Shock your brain into reset mode

Ginger, onion, lemon, naga chilli. Assaulting your tastebuds wakes up your brain and jolts you out of a numb or disconnected state.

Media

The skeletons in my closet
Stephen Lewis -TEDx

Dr Stephen Lewis was 15 when he first started harming. Describing himself as having a supportive family and being a pretty normal teenager, it was not until he suffered bullying that life changed. Now the co-Founder of Self-injury Outreach and Support, Dr Lewis' story is personal, honest and affirming that change can happen when we reach out for it.

Be more Rocky
Watch the movie and then join a boxing club

Rocky is a legend and Sly Stallone is the epitome of physical and mental resilience. Sharmaine in the MeeTwo office is a huge fan. HUGE. We rate boxing because it makes you physically strong, but it also helps combat depression and anxiety. Boxing requires complete concentration and intense effort so for self-harmers, it provides the ideal combination of 100% physical and mental engagement. Unlike self harm, boxing is pain with gain.

Spreading Hope With Butterflies
Alexa Chavarry, TEDx

Alexa was a teenager when she came up with the the Butterfly Project (see activities). She was depressed, suicidal and self harming, but what began as a personal coping strategy soon became an inspiration to help others.

Support

Childline

Phone, text and online support with trained counsellors

You can talk about ANYTHING and have a 1-2-1 chat with a trained counsellor through their website.

24 Hour helpline: 0800 1111

Kooth

Kooth offers free, safe, anonymous support

Only available in certain areas of the UK. Different age limitations apply depending on where you live.

Online counselling service

Monday to Friday, 12pm to 10pm
Saturday to Sunday, 6pm to 10pm, with moderated forums and self-help articles accessible at any time.

The Mix

Free Helpline: 0808 808 4994

Free Crisis Text Line THEMIX 85258

1-2-1 Chat is available on the website Sunday to Friday, 11am to 11pm, Saturday, from 8pm to 11pm.

HeadMeds

Find out more about your medications.

HeadMeds does not give you medical advice but it can fill you in on what different meds are used for and flag up possible side effects.

Self-Help

The Depression Alliance (Mind)

60 self-help groups nationwide

They also run Friends in Need, an online community and its wellbeing network.

Mind

Information Line

Their website contains a very detailed A to Z Guide of Mental Health and information and support which you can access for free.

Infoline: 0300 123 3393

Friday, 9 am to 6 pm

Mental Health and Growing Up

Royal College Of Psychiatrists

Downloadable factsheet with advice and information for young people and parents.

The Blurt Foundation

Self-Care Starter Kit

This free starter kit will help you to look after yourself from the inside and out. They also have Buddy Boxes, known as a 'hug in a box' which you can subscribe to monthly.

Apps

Cove

Create music to express feelings

Free, personal musical journal to help you with your emotional and mental health. Trusted by the NHS.

Reflectly

Diary app

How you are feeling on a daily basis matters. Reflectly is a personal journal and diary driven by artificial intelligence to enable you to deal with negative thoughts, make positivity louder and to teach you about the science of wellbeing. Free, with a premium option.

Happy Not Perfect

Supported by science. Designed by people

Includes simple exercises to boost mental wellbeing, a quick 7-step routine to help you boost your feel-good hormones and relax your nervous system.

What's Up

Cognitive Behavioral Therapy techniques

Using a mixture of Cognitive Behavioural Therapy and Acceptance Commitment Therapy, What's Up uses a positive and negative habit tracker to help users keep up with good habits and ditch those that are counterproductive.

Books

Reasons to Stay Alive
Matt Haig

An accessible and life-affirming memoir of Haig's struggle with depression, and how his triumph over the illness taught him to live.

REASONS
TO STAY
ALIVE
Matt Haig

Prozac Nation
Elizabeth Wurtzel

Seminal book on being young and depressed. Wurtzel explains how it feels to have depression. She survived it. You can too!

It's Kind of a Funny Story
Ned Vizzini

A book that makes you realize there will be people out there who understand what you're going through.

F*** Depression
Robert Duff PhD.

Psychologist Robert Duff's practical and humourous guide to solving the issues caused by depression.

Boy Meets Depression
Or life sucks and then you live

Through the lens of his own near suicide, Kevin Breel's book explores what it's like to be young, male, and depressed in a culture that has no place for that.

Activities

Exercise
Run the pain away

Any form of physical activity prompts the release of feel good chemicals in the brain which help to boost mood and ease symptoms of depression. Even taking a short walk outside in the fresh air helps.

STEM4 Friends

If you're worried about a friend or family member being depressed, STEM4 has a step by step guide on how to approach them

The inverse traffic light rule:

Green = Talk, Amber = Listen, Red = Act

Volunteer
Help yourself by helping others

Volunteering can ease depression and increase a sense of wellbeing and satisfaction. Many mental health organisations such as Mind have volunteering opportunities.

Educate Your Peers
Speak out about mental health

Create a mental health pinboard in your school or set up a young leaders group to change attitudes to mental health. Or make a YouTube video. Watch The Stand Up Kid from Time To Change to see how young people affected by mental health problems in the West Midlands made a difference.

Media

My mental health is a positive part of me
Owen Jones meets Olly Alexander

The lead singer from Years and Years talks about his mental health struggles.

Inside Out
Disney Pixar

An animated movie shows a simple yet effective way of explaining some of our emotions and encourages the need to express how we feel, not just to others, but also to ourselves.

I had a black dog, his name was depression
YouTube

Created by the World Health Organisation and based on the book by Matthew Johnstone, this short animation is about fighting depression and the importance of seeking help.

I Had a Black Dog

Support

No Panic

For 13 to 20 year olds.

Talk to a counsellor about panic or anxiety.

Youth Helpline: 0330 606 1174

Monday to Friday, 3pm to 6pm

Thursday, 6pm to 8pm

Saturday, 6pm to 8pm

Breathe Line: 01952 680835

A recording explaining the breathing technique if you are having a panic attack.

Anxiety UK

Run by volunteers who have lived with anxiety, stress and depression

They can help you deal with anxiety and panic as well as specific phobias such as fear of spiders, blushing, vomiting, being alone, public speaking, heights or any fear that is stopping you get on with your life.

Infoline: 03444 775 774

Mon-Fri, 9:30am - 5.30pm

CAMHS: Anxiety & Stress

Child and Adolescent Mental Health Services

Information on the different kinds of anxiety that can affect young people. Read Emma Selby's interview in the Expert section for more details.

Self-Help

Just Breathe

Calming breathing technique

If you're sitting or standing, place both feet flat on the ground, roughly hip-width apart. Breathe in gently and count steadily from one to five. Then, without pausing or holding your breath, let the air flow out gently, counting from five back down to one. Keep doing this for three to five minutes.

Moodjuice

Moodjuice Scotland Anxiety Guide

Download this NHS worksheet with detailed information on how to help yourself manage anxiety. Terrible layout and dreadful graphics but extremely helpful information.

Gravity Anxiety Blankets

A great big hug from a blanket

The Gravity anxiety blanket is made up of small square sections that are filled with glass micro-beads, which allows the weight to be distributed evenly over your body. The cheapest one costs £149 but fans insist they help them to feel calmer.

Laugh about it all

@introvertdoodles on Instagram

@gemmacorrell on Twitter/Insta

@sow_ay on Tumblr/Insta/Twitter

Check these out on the web too

Engrish.com

awkwardfamilyphotos.com

boredpanda.com

Apps

Wysa Happiness Chabot

A cute penguin who wants to cheer you up

Wysa helps to build emotional resilience by talking to you about your situation. Over 60 psychologists and 10,000 users have provided specific inputs to shape how Wysa helps them.

MindShift™ App

Helps teens cope with anxiety

Strategies and tools to help you deal with everyday anxiety. We like typing our worries and then setting them on fire.

Smiling Mind

Mindfulness meditation

Free app developed by psychologists and educators specifically for young people. We like it because it is 100% not for profit and the meditations are tailored by age from 7-18.

I Love Hue

Ombré for the anxious

Pointless, yet compelling app. When your world feels out of control, creating simple visual harmonies from mosaic tiles is strangely soothing.

Books

Finding Audrey
Sophie Kinsella

Funny, witty, heartwarming, well-researched novel about a bullied 14 year old girl with social anxiety.

What You Must Think of Me
A first-hand Account of one teenager's experience with social anxiety disorder.

Emily Ford's personal story, written with psychiatrist Michael Liebowitz is available to download as a PDF.

Hyperbole And A Half
Unfortunate situations, flawed coping mechanisms, mayhem, and other things that happened

Allie Brosh is just brilliant, brilliant, brilliant. Trust us

Cringeworthy
A theory of awkwardness

Drawing on often mortifying personal experiences, author Melissa Dahl explains why we cringe, why it can be a good thing and asks whether awkwardness is actually any different from other anxiety emotions.

Activities

Make crunchy slime
Two minute recipe for British crunchy slime

Squelching, crunching sounds trigger an ASMR, or Autonomous Sensory Meridian Response which creates feelings of relaxation.

Ingredients

- PVA or clear glue
- Bicarbonate of Soda or Baking Soda
- Contact Lens Solution. Check that it contains boric acid (borax) as it won't work without it.
- Gel food colouring
- Micro Styrofoam Beads
- Glitter, if you fancy adding a bit of sparkle

Instructions

- Tip one cup of PVA glue into a clean bowl.
- Add one tsp of bicarbonate of soda.
- Mix together and add food colouring.
- Add one tablespoon of contact lens solution.
- Mix until stringy and coming away from the edges of the bowl.
- Knead it between your hands. It will be sticky at first, but within 20 seconds it will firm up and become stretchy.
- If for some reason it's still too sticky then add just a few more drops of contact lens solution. Be careful as too much will result in it becoming brittle and snapping.
- Fold in the styrofoam beads and glitter.
- Enjoy!

Media

Sangu Delle
There is no shame in taking care of your mental health

Delle shares how he learned to handle his anxiety in a society that's uncomfortable with emotions. He says "being honest about how we feel doesn't make us weak – it makes us human."

When I worry about things
Mosaic Films - BBC

Personal stories, voiced by the young person but animated beautifully. Worth watching.

Laurel Braitman
Animal madness

Compulsive bears, cats with OCD, depressed dogs, self-destructive rats, what can we earn from animal mental health issues?

Simone Giertz
Useless Robots

Simone's robots rarely (if ever) succeed but making useless robots turns off that voice in your head that tells you that you know exactly how the world works.

The MeeTwo
Teenage Mental Help
Handbook

We'd like to say a huge thank you to all the amazing young people from across the UK who are currently using the MeeTwo app. Listening to you and learning more about what you need has been the inspiration for this handbook Without you, none of this would have been possible.

Sales & Marketing
Sharmaine Malik

Youth Engagement and Fundraising
Kerstyn Comley
Thomas Freeney

Press
Hilly Janes

Schools and Universities
Mulberry UTC, Tower Hamlets
Churston Ferrers Grammar School, Devon
London College of Communication,
University of the Arts London
Park High School, Middlesex
Sylvia Young Theatre School, London

Sponsors
The Texel Foundation
Teach First
Santander
EXPO Live

Supporters
Mermaids
Kooth
Humane Engineering
Gendered Intelligence
Family Planning Association
Ipnos Software Inc
Neybox Digital Ltd
Osborne Cawkwell
Educational Consultants
Flo Health Inc
The Sleep Council

Published by MeeTwo Education Ltd
Printed in the United Kingdom by Park Communications
First Printing, 2018

ISBN 978-1-9164959-9-9

Editor & Creative Director
Suzi Godson
Assistant
Scarlet Evans

Photography
Freddie Marriage
Katy English
Scarlet Evans
Ellen Pearson
Alexander Kireev
Eugenia Maximo
Suzi Godson
Stroma Cairns
Bebeplace
Creative Commons
Unsplash
Pixabay

Illustrations
Yumi Sakagawa
Katie Lennard
Katie Jordan
Josie Chiswell Jones
Dinah Hall
Ruby Evans
Amber Evans
Velvet Lowe

Yumi Sakagawa illustrations are excerpted from her beautiful books 'Your Illustrated Guide to Becoming One With the Universe' and 'There is No Right Way to Meditate' Copyright © 2014 & 2015 by Yumi Sakugawa and published by Adams Media, a division of Simon and Schuster, Inc. Used with permission of the publisher. All rights reserved.

Transcription
Isobel Hewitt

Proofreading
Rachel Carlyle

Interns
Lydia Torrington
Urvi & Adrea

Supreme Patience
Tim Lowe
Ian Comley

We've done our best, but if you do find a typo in this publication, do us a huge favour and email us at info@meetwo.co.uk

In the last ten years, there has been a six fold increase in the number of you who are struggling with mental health issues. The statistics are alarming. One in four 14 year old girls has symptoms of depression. The incidence of self-harm has doubled and suicide is now the leading cause of death in young people; 70% are boys.

We think you deserve more information about why this is happening. In this section you can read interviews with some of the UK's top psychiatrists, neuroscientists, economists and academics who explain what might be going on now and what needs to change to make you feel better.

The first print run of The MeeTwo Mental Help Handbook was funded by a Kickstarter campaign. Without the support of everyone on this list, it would never have been produced. Their generosity means that young people across the country now have access to this unique resource.

Karen Hanton
Nigel Bliss
Don & Julie Godson
Adrian Court
Ian Nairn
Isamaya ffrench
Kim Morrish
Liberty Global Group
Pat Wheeler Jones
Simon Tuttle

Æthan French
Alex
Athena Paginton
Bea McIntosh
Becky Schutt
Ben Clarke
Benedicte Gercke
Bridget Connell
Caroline Morton
Caroline Wagstaff
Cathy Taylor
Celia Briggs
Chris Dyson
Chris Mott
Clare Singleton
Clement Camilleri
David Wilkinson
Dorian McFarland
Elizabeth
Elizabeth Cooper
Elizabeth Wilson
Erica Wolfe-Murray
F Kramer
Fiona Colquhoun
Fran Needham
Frances Torrington
Inaki Izcue
J Chevallier
Janita Tan
Jayne Simpson
Jemma Lawley
Jenni Newcombe
Jennifer Singer
Jenny Baggs

Jessica Dimbleby
Jonathan Pryce
Jill Reidy
Josine Sahakian
Ju Yen Tan
Jules Pancholi
Julie Weeds
K Riegler
Kathryn
Kathy Coach
Laura Mills
Laura Ronchini
Lauren Wilson
Lesley Annand
Lidka Semetilo
Michael Gorgy
Michael Norton
Michael Wilson
Mike Jenkinson
Moritz Platt
Neil Johnson
Nibs Webber
Nicholas Hillen
NIPS
Omer Moghraby
Paul Summerfield
Ross Taylor
Ruby Evans
Sandy Foskett
Sophie Brandon
Sophie Lidbetter
starmaru
Stef and Alice Mastropietro
Susie Atkinson
Susie Schutt
The Creative Fund
Thomas Freeney
Tim Ryder
Tim Spence
Tosh Kojima
Tracey Essery
Verena Hewat
Verity Bramwell
Zoe Berger

EXPERT ANALYSIS

B6. Expert Overview
Sir Simon Wessely
President of the Royal Society of Medicine,
Regius Professor of Psychiatry, Kings College, London

B12. Social Influence
Sarah-Jayne Blakemore
Professor of Cognitive Neuroscience, UCL.
Author of 'Inventing Ourselves: The Secret Life of The Teenage Brain'

B16. Happiness
Lord Richard Layard
Emeritus Professor of Economics, LSE
Co-founder of Action for Happiness

B20. CAMHS Explained
Emma Selby
Clinical nurse specialist and digital pioneer

B26. Self-harm & Suicide
David Gunnell
Professor of Epidemiology, University of Bristol
Member of the National Suicide Prevention Advisory Group

B35. Social Media
Suzi Godson
Research psychologist and author
Co-founder of MeeTwo Education

B42. Addiction
Henriettta Bowden-Jones
Consultant psychiatrist in addictions
Vice President of the Medical Women's Federation

B49. Education
Sir Anthony Seldon
Vice-Chancellor, The University of Buckingham
Co-founder of Action for Happiness

THE MENTAL HELP DIRECTORY

This directory has been designed to give you the tools to help yourself, no matter what the problem is. Each double page spread lists useful and effective support groups, helplines, apps, books, self-help and media, as well as fun activities that can help you to feel better.

PERSONAL STORIES

My Valentines 8c

Roses are red,
Violets are blue,
I drop down like dead
when Im not with You

Please see me.

"Please See Me"
Teacher's note illustrating the hypervigilance that exists around student mental health in the education system.

Expert Analysis.

A new understanding of teenage mental health issues.

Sir Simon Wessely

**President of the
Royal Society of Medicine.
Regius Professor of Psychiatry,
Kings College, London.**

**Do we worry about mental health more than
we used to?** Worrying about mental health issues
is nothing new. Throughout history people have
been convinced that children are more stressed,
parents are more useless, exams are more difficult
and jobs are harder to get. However, when boffins
like me try to measure whether anything has
actually changed, we usually find that the rates of
all mental health problems are remarkably static.

That has changed. In the last few years we have
seen a genuine rise in the levels of anxiety in
young women aged 18 to 24. We haven't done
enough research with children and teenagers yet,
but we expect that we will see the same thing in
younger people too. It is a significant increase.

**About 25 percent of young women now
have a recognisable anxiety disorder, and as
a psychiatrist, I think that number is
worryingly high.**

What do you think has caused it? Lots of people have an opinion on what might have caused this change. At the moment everyone says "oh it must be social media", but that might be because technological change makes them feel uneasy. If you go back and look at the history of printing, or newspapers, or the telegraphy, or the television, you will find exactly the same thing.

It is never a good idea to speculate, but if I were to hazard a guess, I would say that social media is the medium, not the message, and that it is not the cause of the current rise in anxiety disorders. The rise in debt and tuition fees could also play a part, except that Scottish students don't pay tuition fees and yet there has also been a similar rise in student mental health problems in Scotland.

Have we become too risk averse? Have we brought our kids up in a way that prevents them from becoming independent? We don't let kids walk to school anymore and the distance parents let children play away from the house has shrunk dramatically. This could mean that when finally kids leave home, they are not as well prepared as they might have been previously.

Does the media play a part? The media's ability to hype up a problem is nothing new, but I suspect most people learn how to filter it out from quite an early age. If anything, the fact that there is so much news now means that we pay very little attention to it. More is less, in that sense.

We've also seen a rise in psychiatric disorders like post-traumatic stress disorder, which is a result of trauma. Have we become more violent as a society? Is there more sexual violence? Possibly, but the real answer is we don't know. The only thing we do know is that something has changed and this is a rougher, harder time, for this particular age group.

What about raised awareness? There's no question that levels of awareness of mental health problems have gone up in the population, but this can sometimes be a two edged sword. Being able to use social media to seek support, or admit that you feel down, or anxious, or that you have concerns about your sexuality, is a good thing, but it is equally important to be able to distinguish between the normal emotions that make us feel human, and conditions that are clinical and require treatment.

We all have 'mental health'; it's like breathing, or blood pressure. Everybody is sad at times, everybody gets moody, everybody has good days, or bad days, or feels anxious before an exam, or devastated by bereavement, or divorce, but it's important to emphasise that these are normal emotional responses.

Good and bad days are not a mental health problem. Getting high and then getting very low and wanting to harm or kill yourself, that's a disorder, and it's important that we don't confuse the two.

Has there been an increase in self-harm? Rates of self-harm are going up. That's partly because we are now classifying things such as drinking a bottle of vodka as self-harm. It is harmful and it is you hurting yourself, so it is 'self-harm', but changing the definition has meant that the rates have gone up.

Self-harm is a complicated issue. People who cut, for example, experience a sense of relief when they do it. It's not a great way of making yourself feel better, but nor is it necessarily an attempt to kill yourself and it's not always a mental health issue.

In cultures which practice scarification, it can be normal. I personally don't like it, but then I don't like tattoos and they are very culturally normal too. Nevertheless, rates of deliberate self-harm have increased in young people, that's still true.

How do you decide whether a young person needs treatment? It is a judgment call based on the level of distress, the severity of the action itself and the things going on around it. When we study these things, we find that most people get through, even very tough times, if they have a supportive social network.

We also know that getting a diagnosis of a mental health problem is not always a good thing. It can change the way you view yourself by making you believe that there is something more fundamentally wrong with you, as opposed to a temporary difficult time.

You might end up thinking that you are someone who will always be unable to handle stress, or be 'vulnerable', and be heading for a lifetime of trouble. Perhaps so, but perhaps not. And all treatments have side effects – it's not just drugs like antidepressants, but even things like counselling.

How can talking therapies be harmful? Talking therapies can make you too introspective and sometimes you can have bad experiences with therapists. You can become dependent on counselling, although not in the same way that you can become dependent on drugs and alcohol. And they can make you worse.

We've done a lot of work on how people respond to major traumas such as the Manchester bombing, or the London bombs a few years ago and we found that most people got better in their own time. But we know that people who had a particular form of counselling, known as "psychological debriefing" within 24 hours of the incident actually felt worse.

Perhaps it was too little, and too early, at a time when you really don't need to be reminded of just how awful an incident was – that can wait till later. Or perhaps it got in the way of doing what comes naturally, who knows? We have to be careful about not over pathologising ordinary behaviour, but we also have to consider reverse incentives.

For example, if a teacher gets handed a difficult class, they just have to get on with it, but if one of those children has a psychiatric label, the teacher is more likely to be able to call on classroom support, so often, we find teachers pushing psychiatrists to diagnose things like ADHD, or Autism, when the psychiatrist just doesn't think that's the case.

There's a lot of pressure from the parents too. When a child is constantly misbehaving in public places, or just letting the side down, and they feel that everyone is blaming them, it really helps if they can say "oh no, it's, you know, Toby has got, whatever the diagnosis is", and then everyone goes "ahhhh, that's so sad".

I sympathise with why this happens, both for teachers and parents, and I know full well that getting the right diagnosis for something like Autism or ADHD can be immensely liberating for all concerned because it enables help to be provided – but the key word here is "right diagnosis".

Giving people the wrong diagnosis is as harmful as missing the right diagnosis.

What can we do to protect mental health in young people? After parents, the most important structure in a child's life is their school and their teachers. We did a great study with the British army in Afghanistan going out to the forward bases and checkpoints beyond the big bases like Bastion and Lashkar Gah looking at mental health there. What we showed was that the actions of the Taliban were a smaller determinant of mental health in a unit compared to measures of leadership and group cohesion.

I have never seen a study like this of head teachers, but the military and educational establishments are more similar than you might think, and I am now going to bet my merit award that if you were to do this study in schools, you would find that the best way to protect mental health in young people would be to provide strong leadership, support your staff, and create strong group cohesion within the schools.

X 20 Sunday I went to Arts
Centre (by myself!) in
yellow cords r blouse.
Ian was there but
he didn't speak to
me. Got little rhyme put
in my handbag from
someone who's apparently
got a crush on me. Its
~~watched man told on moon~~

X 21 Monday Went to village.
Later went to town
with Zoé r Anne. Got
a short sleeved shirt.
Saw Jim r Zoé said
hello to him but he
thought it was me!
~~Had tea in town.~~
Went to village again.
Roger came r stayed night.
He'd hurt his elbow.

Went to v
mostly for
tomorrow.
Fraser's wa
He blew m
███ I g
embarasse
used to him
polio vacc
Roger stayed
else

Zoé wen
Paris. M
to town.
lovely.
materi a
to make
dresses
an. Remb
one. Kem

"I went to arts centre (by myself!)
in yellow cords & blouse.
Ian was there but he didn't speak to me.
Got little rhyme put in my handbag
from someone who's apparently
got a crush on me.
It's Nicholas I think. UGH!
Watched man land on moon."

Diary entry for Sunday, 20th July, written by Dinah Hall in 1969
Original diary pictured left

Sarah-Jayne Blakemore

Professor of Cognitive Neuroscience
University College London.
Author of 'Inventing Ourselves: The
Secret Life Of The Teenage Brain'.

Why is adolescence such an important stage in our development? On the previous page is a diary entry from a teenage girl which was written in 1969. It reads...

"I went to arts centre (by myself!) in yellow cords & blouse. Ian was there but he didn't speak to me. Got little rhyme put in my handbag from someone who's apparently got a crush on me. It's Nicholas I think. UGH! Watched man land on moon."

This beautifully illustrates what really matters to a teenage girl: what she's wearing, who she likes, or doesn't like, is so much more important than the fact that man has just landed on the moon.

Adolescence is the period of life in which we develop our sense of self-identity, particularly our sense of our social self, that is how other people see us. In the teenage years, how you represent yourself to the outside world and how other people see you, takes on a step-change in importance.

That's not to say you don't have self awareness before adolescence, of course you do, but how you're seen by other people becomes particularly important, and that's why, during the teenage years we start to really care about the music we listen to and our fashion tastes, and what peer group we hang out with, who we like, who we don't like, even things like our political beliefs and our moral beliefs take a step change in importance because we are developing our sense of self.

The teenage years are when we begin to become independent from our families. That's the whole point of adolescence, to eventually end up as an independent adult, and we achieve that by inventing ourselves and developing our sense of who we are.

What behaviours are most typical of teenagers? A typical adolescent behaviour is self-consciousness. There is this sense of embarrassment which seems to come online in the teenage years, particularly embarrassment in front of your parents. For example, I have a ten-year-old and a thirteen-year-old and I'm a governor at their school. I recently had to visit both the primary and the secondary and their reaction characterises the difference between those two stages of development. My ten-year-old said "oh brilliant, can I organise it? I want to show you around" and my thirteen-year-old looked completely horrified and said, very politely, "would you mind if I pretended not to know who you are?"

There is something very physiological about this sense of self consciousness in adolescents. An interesting study by Leah Sommerville at Harvard tested this by putting children, teenagers and adults in a brain scanner and recording their brain activity. The study involved looking at very boring screens, but occasionally, she told the participants that there was someone of about the same age as them in the scanner room and that they were going to be observing their face in the scanner. They were told that they would know when they were being observed because a little red light would come on.

It was just a cover story. There was never anyone else in the scanner room, but when they thought they were being watched, self-reported levels of embarrassment were highest in adolescents, compared to children and adults. Adolescents also had more sweat on their skin, which is another measure of stress, than adults or children, and higher levels of activity in the social brain network than adults.

Another typical adolescent behaviour is risk taking so we worry about things like smoking and drinking, experimenting with drugs and dangerous driving. Dangerous driving is a particular case in point.

A recent UK report found that that drivers between the ages of 17 and 24 make up only 7% of British licence holders, yet they cause 85% of all serious accidents.

It is important to point out that not all adolescents take risks and there are lots of individual differences. It's also true that risk is often positive but we tend to focus on the negative ones. It's really important to take risks in lots of domains, like in academic life, like putting up your hand to answer a question, or guessing an answer to a test question. Risk taking in those situations is useful and we can learn from it. It is also important to understand the context of risk taking for young people.

If you think about smoking, drinking and drug taking, adolescents who take those risks are not normally doing those things on their own. They normally take those risks when they're with their friends.

The social context of risk taking is really critical. It was demonstrated very neatly by Larry Steinberg and his colleagues in a lab based experiment using a video arcade driving game. He looked at the number of risks people took while driving the circuit. In the game it was possible to break an amber light to save time and win points but if the light turned red before you cleared it you crashed and lost points. What Steinberg found was that young people drove as carefully as adults when they were on their own, but in a second condition, Steinberg asked the participants to bring some friends with them and they stood behind the participants while they were driving.

When young people had friends with them, 13-16 years olds took around three times the number of risks and 17-24 year olds took around twice as many.

Research by car insurance companies using real life data from accidents finds the same thing. These findings are now informing policy and in some countries, young people are not allowed to carry any passengers, except family members, in the car with them for a certain amount of time after they pass their test. Similarly, some car insurance companies are offering reduced premiums for younger people as long as they do not take any passengers in their car.

Is there a way to harness the importance of peer power in a positive way? Yes. It is helpful to view teenage risk-taking through the lens of social influence and what we know about being ostracised or excluded from a peer group. Many parents and teachers say that they don't understand why intelligent, well-educated young people go out on the weekend and do apparently 'stupid' things like experiment with drugs, alcohol and cigarettes.

However, if you think about those decisions in terms of social risk, you see them in a more rational light. In the heat of the moment, adolescents might care more about avoiding the social risk of being excluded by their peers, than other kinds of risks such as health risks, or legal risks.

If an intelligent educated thirteen-year-old goes out at the weekend and is offered a cigarette by her friends, what to her is the bigger risk? Saying yes to a cigarette, when she knows it carries a long term health risk, or that she might be caught, or saying no and potentially being ostracised by her peer group right now. For a teenager, the risk of immediate social isolation seems to be more powerful than the risk of long term health issues, or being told off by a parent.

This understanding suggests we ought to change the way we challenge teenage decision making and perhaps we should change the way we present public health messages and advertising aimed at this age group.

If you think about the way health advertising is currently aimed at young people, it is almost always focused on the long term health risks of behaviours like smoking, or binge drinking, or dangerous driving, when in fact there's evidence to suggest that, that this age group cares more about the social norms and what their friends are thinking and doing, than long term health consequences.

Other public health research is exploring what happens when teenagers deliver messages to each other. A few years ago a US research group worked with 56 middle schools with children aged 12 to 15. Half of the schools carried out an anti-bullying campaign run by the teachers and the other half of the schools carried similar anti-bullying campaigns run by the students themselves. In those schools in which the campaigns were

led by the children, there was a 30% decrease in bullying behaviour and a significant change in bullying attitudes, compared with the schools where similar anti-bullying campaigns were carried out by teachers.

So, if you want to change young people's behaviour to make it safer, for example, and more pro-social, then focusing on the young people's views and attitudes will probably work better in the long term than focusing on long term risks, which are less meaningful to them at this point in their lives.

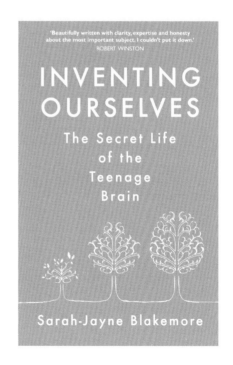

'Beautifully written with clarity, expertise and honesty about the most important subject. I couldn't put it down.'
ROBERT WINSTON

INVENTING OURSELVES

The Secret Life
of the
Teenage
Brain

Sarah-Jayne Blakemore

Lord Richard Layard

Emeritus Professor of Economics, London School of Economics. Co-founder of Action for Happiness.

You are an economist, so how did you become interested in mental health?
Actually, my parents were Jungian psychoanalysts and I thought about becoming a psychiatrist when I was a student, so I've always had an interest it. And there is an economic argument for my interest in mental health too.

Mental health issues cost the UK economy at least £70 billion in lost output and a further £10 billion in extra physical healthcare. If you have a physical illness and you also have a mental illness, you will get fifty percent more treatment from the NHS for your physical illness because you keep on going to A&E.

If you are treating children and adolescents with mental illness, the economic savings tend to come a bit later on, but half of adult mental health issues present by the age of 14 and if these problems don't get addressed when they're manageable, they become entrenched.

People develop incredible strategies for hiding their problems and the shocking thing is that very few of those who need it get any help and fewer still get the help they need. That's not necessarily because there's been an increase in mental health problems. It is mainly a resource problem and the failure to organise it all properly.

What can we do to improve that? The situation with children now is exactly the same as it was ten years ago. There is no treatment available unless you're at the extreme end of desperation and the Child and Adolescent Mental Health Services (CAMHS) threshold has been rising all the time. Theresa May has said that mental health is a top priority, so we lobbied for last year's green paper and it has three recommendations which will make a real difference.

The first is that we will have Mental Health Support Teams with good clinical leads in every area. That's going to take time because you would be lucky to find 200 clinical leads in the whole country at the moment. We also want to see CAMHS upgraded and waiting lists reduced. And finally, we want to have a trained mental health teacher to identify cases and make the pupils and teachers more conscious of mental health issues.

Is that ambitious? We have made it work with adults. The NHS has in recent years developed a totally new service to deliver evidence-based psychological therapies. It's called Improving Access to Psychological Therapies (IAPT). This service has, over six years, trained 6,000 therapists and is now treating six hundred thousand people a year, with a recovery rate of 50% and rising.

The most studied therapy is CBT – Cognitive Behavioural Therapy, which is a broad heading for therapies which focus on directly influencing thoughts and behaviours – in order to affect the quality of human experience. In hundreds of randomised controlled trials CBT has been shown to produce recovery rates of over 50% for depression and anxiety disorders.

The net cost of providing these treatments is zero because they save so much money in disability benefits, crime, social services and additional physical healthcare.

When did you start thinking about the economic case for 'happiness'? About 18 years ago I wrote my book 'Happiness: Lessons from a New Science' and I realised that the thing we can do, most readily, to reduce unhappiness in the world, and in our society, is to deal with mental health problems.

Depression and anxiety disorders are the biggest single cause of misery in Western societies. When you run the equation on data measuring things like income, education, unemployment, relationships or physical health, mental health always comes through as the most important factor in unhappiness.

We have evidence to show that happiness and fulfilment come less from material wealth and more from relationships; less from focussing on ourselves and more from helping others; less from external factors outside our control and more from the way in which we choose to react to what happens to us.

What do you think are the main pressures on young people? I think the educational system has definitely become more stressful. I think that social media is very important. Jean Twenge's research in the USA shows that with mental health, everything goes to pot after about 2010. The issues appear to be worse for young women and I have just been looking at some data which suggests that thirteen percent of women aged sixteen to twenty-four have made a suicide attempt at some point.

Some people dismiss issues like anxiety and panic attacks as attention seeking? That has been used as an argument for not helping people in a really serious situation. I don't think it is helpful to tell someone who is suffering or is worried that they have a condition that there is nothing wrong with them. A lot of Freudians think diagnosis is bad, but I think people find it very helpful. Having a diagnosis means that something can be done for them and that is very important. There is a big difference between being diagnosed and being diagnosable. The last really big study which looked at the Mental Health of Children and Young People in Great Britain, in 2004, surveyed children in their own homes.

That research suggested that ten percent of children between five and sixteen would be diagnosed with anxiety if they ever sought treatment; however, only a quarter of those children were actually getting the help they needed.

What can young people do to help themselves? In 2010 we set up a movement called Action for Happiness to promote practical action for a happier, more caring society. Action for Happiness has been more active with adults than with children, but we would love more young people to get involved and we have produced some rather nice materials for children including the book '50 Ways To Feel Happy' which was written by Vanessa King. There are also some good resources for parents on the website.

Ten Keys For Happiness

From Action For Happiness

The ten keys for happy living are based on a review of the latest research from psychology. Practicing them has a positive impact on people's happiness and wellbeing and they are as useful to children and teenagers as they are to adults.

The first five keys are about how we interact with the outside world in daily activities.

Giving. Do things for others. Do three extra acts of kindness today. Try to bring a smile to others.

Relating. Connect with other people. Make more time for the people who really matter to you.

Exercising. Take care of your body. Notice which healthy actions lift your mood and do more of them.

Appreciating. Notice the world around. Stop and take five minutes to just breathe and be in the moment.

Trying out. Keep learning new things. Learn a new skill, however small.

The second five keys come from inside us and depend on our attitude to life.

Direction. Have goals to look forward to. Think of a goal you're aiming for and do one thing to get it started.

Resilience. Find ways to bounce back. Share how you really feel with someone you trust. Be willing to ask for help.

Emotion. Take a positive approach. Smile and say something positive every time you walk into a room.

Acceptance. Be comfortable with who you are. Be as kind to yourself as you are to others.

Meaning. Be part of something bigger than you. Volunteer and give your time to support a good cause.

www.actionforhappiness.org

Emma Selby

Clinical Nurse Specialist,
North East London Foundation Trust.
Digital pioneer and creator of the
MindFresh app.

Why do you think there has been an increase in mental health issues in young people? It has never been as hard to be a teenager as it is right now. It doesn't stop at the end of the school day any more. Bullying is 24/7. Pressures are 24/7. We have thirteen-year olds who are panicking about how they're going to get into university when they've only just got into secondary school! Some of it is down to parents. Twenty years ago, no one knew what Cognitive Behavioural, Therapy was, but now we get parents demanding it for their kids. I've had parents chasing bereavement counselling for their son because his grandfather died eight days earlier and he was very sad. He should be. It's perfectly normal for a child to be sad because somebody has died. Call me if he is sad in a year.

It is partly because parents are so much more aware of mental health issues and they are also aware of what treatments are available. Doctor Google has a lot to answer for! They go to the GP knowing what they want. Often a GP has only five or 10 minutes to make a judgement call, so when a parent is being really demanding, they take the easy option and put that referral through to us.

Parents wrongly think that mental health services are a quick fix. They are not. In fact they don't fix anything. When you break your leg the plaster cast doesn't fix your leg. Your leg fixes itself. Mental health services are exactly the same. We don't fix young people's mental health problems. Young people fix them, by getting better at coping with the stresses around them. They might need the support of their parents and teachers to do that, and we might provide some counselling services to help keep them safe while they're learning to build those skills, but essentially, they are the ones doing all the fixing.

Do you think that parents are pathologising normal emotions? I think it was a mistake to pay so much attention to the stigma around mental health issues, without making it clear that a certain amount of stress and emotional fluctuation is normal. There is no point running campaigns that tell you it is fine to talk about something, if you don't then provide people with the information that they need in order to be able to differentiate between a normal emotional experience and one that is clinical.

There was a campaign recently where young people were talking about the symptoms of bipolar. After it, there was a huge leap in young people googling the words "do I have bipolar." They'd seen campaigns and thought that sounds like me, so I must have bipolar. No you are not bipolar. You are just fourteen and hormonal. It is only when these issues impact on a young persons ability to thrive that they need mental health services.

The language we use to describe normal emotions doesn't help. Anxiety is a prime example. Twelve years ago anxiety was a diagnostic label. Now we use it as readily as saying I'm a bit tearful, or I'm sad. If we feel sad, we say we are depressed. I think it is confusing for young people.

Why is CAHMS so complicated? The challenge with CAHMS is that the door is shaped differently and it has a different lock on it, depending where you live in the country. For example, if you live in Essex and you're fourteen and you're feeling a bit low, you can call a 'single point of access' phone number, where you can self-refer. You can pick up the phone and talk to a mental health nurse, or a mental health social worker and they'll have a chat about how you're feeling. However, only some CAMHS services accept referrals directly from parents, or children, so we advise young people to go through school or a GP because at least that way, we know their referral will be looked at.

Schools are also a good option because finding the right CAMHS number to call can be a challenge. You would think NHS 111 would have all of those numbers, but they don't. If you are trying to find support in Essex or Hertfordshire, for example, you need to google 'Hertfordshire Single Point of Access' which, if you shorten it down to SPA brings up all kinds of interesting responses! Because most mental health services are obliged to send a report to schools and counsellors once a term to let them know what services they are running, schools tend to have the right contact details.

To add to the confusion, lots of children's mental health services are not even called CAMHS. In Essex for example, young people decided that they didn't like the word CAHMS, so where I work is called EWMHS, which stands for Emotional Wellbeing Mental Health Service. It means you can't even guarantee that googling CAHMS is going to get you to the right phone number. Basically, if we had six children in this room and one lived in Hertfordshire, one lived in Essex and the others were from North London, South London, Kent and Yorkshire, every single one of them would give a different explanation of their CAHMS services because they all work differently.

Because it is so complicated, we always say to children, if you are feeling low, or something's not right, try and get an adult involved, ideally someone from the school because they're the most likely to know what the right local mental health number is. It doesn't have to be your class teacher. We've had referrals from schools that started with the dinner lady, or the cleaner, or the administrator that is at the front desk in the morning, because the child is always two hours late for school and it's always the administrator that lets them in.

How does self-referral work?
In an area where children can self-refer, a mental health worker will have a chat with them over the phone about how they are feeling. They will ask when the feelings started and whether anything specific has triggered them. They will normally ask about risk too. Some young people feel they can't explain what's happening to them over the phone, or they worry that if they say, for example, that they are self-harming, the police are going to be at the door in 40 minutes, but that's obviously not the case. What the mental health nurse is trying to do when they ask about risk is to establish whether that young person is okay to wait a couple of weeks before they see a mental health worker, or whether we need to have a few phone calls with them while they are on the waiting list, just to make sure that they feel we haven't forgotten about them.

We'll generally give them some tips on things that they can do to help themselves while they are on the waiting list. We might advise them to use the MeeTwo app, or if they are self-harming, we can recommend specific apps that might be able to help with that.

If we've had a chat and we think that they're having a difficult time but it's all quite relative and these are really normal feelings to have, we may give them some tools to help them build resilience so they can manage the situation by themselves. We get a lot of these phone calls around exam periods. Children ring up saying "I can't sleep" and "I feel really low" and "I've got no energy during the day", If it's exam period and you are in year 11, you probably don't need to scc a mental health counsellor, but we might give you some tips about turning your electrics off at eight o'clock and having a hot bath, and getting some lavender oil on your pillow.

We'll signpost them to apps and websites or give them advice on things like mindfulness and say to them that if it doesn't help, they should phone back in two weeks and we can have another chat on the phone. We are happy for young people to call us and not meet us at all.

How is that different from calling a helpline? It's completely different because mental health teams are local so they know the area and the school, so they can say "oh yes, it can be a bit stressful at lunch time at your school because the playground is tiny and they let all the years out at the same time". They can also recommend local services. They can say, for example "oh there's a really good charity over there that does mentoring. Why don't you try that?".

When there's been a recent event, or some anti-social behaviour in a certain area and children phone up saying they feel really anxious, you can be more understanding because you have that local knowledge. You can't give that kind of reassurance if you are answering a call from Yorkshire and you are based in central London.

What happens if a child doesn't want their parents to know? It depends on the child's age. If a child is under twelve or thirteen, it's very rare that we would be able to see them without their parents knowing. Nine times out of ten, the letters initially go out to the parents, or carers. If there was an exceptional reason why Mum and Dad shouldn't know, and in some cases there are, we might ask them who else they could bring; a big

sister who's over eighteen, or a teacher they trust, but normally we'd like a parent to be there.

Children above the age of sixteen have the right to not tell their parents, but again, we'd have a conversation with them first so that we can understand why they don't want to tell their parents. We also need to work out if they really understand the implications of not telling their parents what's happening to them and what that could mean for them.

Often the reason young people don't want to tell their parents is that they fear that their parents might judge them, or they might have a really negative view of what's happening for them. Sometimes when we talk that through with them, young people think, actually, maybe I'm not going to be judged and it's alright to tell my parents.

How is CAMHS structured? There are four different tiers in CAMHS. You don't hear people talk about **tier one** in CAHMS because tier one is GP services. Tier two is local counselling services, so for example, school based counsellors, external counsellors who come into the school or local counselling services.

It's what we call low level counselling, where a young person might see somebody with a counselling qualification for six sessions, or they might see somebody who has a mental health qualification. However, a lot of children's mental health services don't actually have tier two anymore because digital is becoming so much more important.

Tier three is a specialist mental health service where we work with young people who may already have a diagnosis, or are meeting a diagnostic threshold. Their issues are either quite severe, or have been going on for a long time. They will get one to one counselling, or they might do group work. In some cases we don't deal directly with the young person, we might deal with the parents, or the school, or the whole family. In tier three you see mental health professionals, so it could be anything from a mental health nurse, to a psychologist to an art therapist or a play therapist. We may begin to discuss medication in tier three, but we'd always have a therapy conversation first.

Tier four is where we look at in-patient admissions. These are the kids who are maybe actively suicidal or psychotic, or have severe eating disorders, or severe OCD; conditions that impact their ability to cope with daily life. Generally speaking a hospital admission can be for about a month or so. Some of them are sectioned, but most are not, and we're increasingly starting to see more and more home treatment teams. We don't have a lot of children's mental health beds, but it's also not good for children to be in mental health hospitals. They need to be at home in a loving environment. The home treatment teams visit daily and nurse them like they're in hospital, but they are in their own home. They still have an assigned doctor and a psychologist or maybe an occupational therapist who sees them regularly.

What is the therapy process like? It's funny. I had a young girl come in to see me recently and she was shocked. She said "you're not old!" They expect me to be this old woman and they think they are going to have to lie down on a couch that's got one arm, like a parody of Freud. Young people think therapy is just sitting and talking but it doesn't have to be that at all. I always ask young people what they want to do in therapy. I have one girl and she doesn't like to make eye contact so we paint each other's nails during therapy sessions. She finds it easier to talk that way. I've got other kids who can't sit still, so we go and kick a ball around, only, whoever's got the ball has to talk.

Do children with serious mental health issues get better? Yes. Children are incredibly resilient and I'd say more children recover than don't. I chose to work in CAHMS because I found that young people have this great gift for recovery, and actually the younger the child is, the faster I've seen them recover.

I love it because I'm starting to get letters and cards and stuff from children who I nursed when I first qualified. One of them sent me a message the other day because she's just started her second year of mental health nursing. I remember her as an in-patient at thirteen, going through this really difficult time, and now she wants to be a mental health nurse in CAHMS.

HANNAH

Scarlet Evans

HEAD MEDS.
STRAIGHT TALK ON MENTAL HEALTH MEDICATION
HeadMeds provides straight-talking advice and information about mental health medication.
visit headmeds.org.uk
Everything you want to know about mental health medication but didn't want to ask.
YOUNGMINDS
fighting for young people's mental health

David Gunnell

**Professor of Epidemiology,
University of Bristol.
Member of the National Suicide
Prevention Advisory Group.**

Is self-harm the same as making a suicide attempt? It's important to be clear what we mean by self-harm and suicide attempts. It's an important distinction. In this country, the term self-harm is often used to cover a very wide range of behaviours, many of which are not motivated by a wish to die. When you talk to people who self-harm, or self-injure, they describe it as being quite separate from making a suicide attempt. They are often going through a really tough time in their lives but, on the whole, they don't self-harm because they want to die. Common reasons people give for self-harm include getting relief from terrible feelings, punishing oneself and showing others how bad you feel.

Only around one in five people who self-harm do so with suicidal intent. But some research indicates self-harming without suicidal intent may be a gateway to making a suicide attempt and a number of people who make suicide attempts have previously self-harmed.

In the US, there's much more of a distinction between non-suicidal and suicidal self-harm. They use the term non-suicidal self-injury to cover any act (most usually self-cutting).

Is self-harm a strong risk factor for suicide?
One of the strongest risk factors for suicide is whether a person has made a previous suicide attempt. About half of the people who die by suicide have attempted suicide previously and around one in twenty people who are admitted to hospital following a suicide attempt will go on to take their own lives over the next 10 years or more. One in five young people in the UK have self-harmed by the age of sixteen, but far fewer have attempted suicide.

Does that prevalence suggest self-harm has become a perverse fashion statement? A lot of people trivialise self harm and say that cutting is attention seeking, but it's usually not. People who self-harm are often really distressed and they are seeking relief from some difficult and distressing feelings. Self-harming without suicidal intent is a strong marker for depression. And since depression and distress can lead to suicide attempts, it's also a risk factor for a suicide attempt.

Even so, most people who self-harm non-suicidally don't go on to make suicide attempts. They are distinct but linked phenomena. Some people do both, but self-harm is very common whereas making a suicide attempt is not.

Surveys indicate that about one in twenty people will make a suicide attempt in their life-time, compared to one in five people or more who engage in non-suicidal self-harm.

Is there a contagion effect with self-harm?
Some people learn coping strategies from other people. This may happen amongst friendship groups who share their coping strategies, it may be through seeing portrayals of self-harm in the media, or young people may go online and see how others use self-injury as a way of coping with their distress. But of course it's not an ideal way of coping with distress. If you're distressed, and self-harm is a signal of that distress, it's better to seek help, talk about it and share your feelings with your friends or your parents or others, rather than keeping it to yourself and injuring yourself.

Why are teenagers so vulnerable to mental health issues? If you look at the incidence of suicide by age, the rates are very much lower amongst children and adolescents than adults, but then throughout puberty, year on year, the incidence of suicide, suicide attempts and self-harm increase.

Many common mental health problems – anxiety, depression, substance misuse – begin around this time too. So many things are happening for young people at this time. Their brains and bodies are maturing, they're becoming independent, they're getting into relationships and they're experiencing the ups and downs that go with relationships for the first time.

Of course we can't wrap young people in cotton wool to protect them from the real world because that's part and parcel of growing up and becoming independent. There's also a challenge

with distinguishing life's up and downs – and their effects on mood - from the onset of mental illness. It's important not to over-medicalise everyday ups and downs in mood, but equally important to identify young people developing mental health problems at an early stage and providing support and treatment. This can be a real challenge.

What is the best treatment? The most important thing is to seek medical advice. On the whole the evidence base for treatment of self-harm in children and teenagers is not as strong as it is for adults, in part because of the ethical challenges around conducting research on children. In adults there is good evidence of the benefits of the talking therapy Cognitive Behavioural Therapy (CBT) although evidence is less clear in children and adolescents. For some high risk groups of adolescents who self-harm there is emerging evidence that Dialectical Behavioural Therapy (DBT) is effective.

What is the best way to help a teenager who is self-harming? First and foremost it's important to seek professional help. When a parent finds out that their child has been self harming or is suicidal it leads to a range of emotions and is usually be bewildering and scary. The first thing they need to do is to take their child to see the GP. The GP will make an assessment and may seek specialist advice from CAHMS. There are a number of good resources online, for example, HealthTalk Online is a nice website where parents talk about their experiences of helping their children who self-harm. The advice to young people is to talk about it. Don't bottle these awful feelings up, talk.

Doesn't talking about suicide makes things worse? The idea that talking about suicide with someone may put the idea into their head is a myth. Asking whether someone is suicidal and talking about suicidal feelings may bring a huge sense of relief to the person experiencing those thoughts.

To have reached a point where you are thinking of ending your life can be the most dreadful feeling and when you're in such severe pain, being able to share with someone it can bring a real sense of relief and, with appropriate support, the starting point on the road to recovery.

Research shows that people who are suicidal may drop hints or refer to the possibility of suicide indirectly, but these may not be taken seriously. Having said that, the way suicide methods are discussed in the media can increase the risk which is why reporting around suicide can be so hazardous. In research we talk about cognitive access, the method a person who is thinking about suicide would use in a moment of crisis.

If a novel method is suggested in the newspapers and it sounds like it would be pain free, someone who is thinking about suicide might decide to try it. This is particularly true of celebrity suicides, or if suicide is glamorised. For example, when Robin Williams died four or five years ago in the States, there was a rapid upturn in suicides, particularly using the method he used.

What percentage of people who think about suicide go on to make a suicide attempt? Thankfully, most people who have suicidal thoughts, do not act on those thoughts and make a suicide attempt. Suicidal thoughts vary in intensity from vague thoughts about life not being worth living all the way up to more concrete planning such as thinking about methods, locations and preparing for their death; such thoughts are clearly much more worrying. People who are depressed and suicidal often feel the world would be better off without them. Their distress may distort the way they think. Many studies have shown the profound and lasting impact that death by suicide has on family, friends, colleagues and communities.

Five Myths About Suicide

Talking about suicide can create or worsen risk. Suicide can be a taboo topic in society. Often, people feeling suicidal don't want to worry or burden anyone with how they feel and so they don't discuss it. By asking directly about suicide you give them permission to tell you how they feel. People who have felt suicidal will often say what a huge relief it is to be able to talk about what they are experiencing. Once someone starts talking they've got a better chance of discovering other options to suicide.

People who talk about suicide aren't serious and won't go through with it. People who kill themselves have often told someone that they do not feel life is worth living or that they have no future. Some may have actually said they want to

die. While it's possible that someone might talk about suicide as a way of getting the attention they need, it's vitally important to take anybody who talks about feeling suicidal seriously.

Most suicides happen suddenly without warning. The majority of suicides have been preceded by warning signs, whether verbal or behavioural. Evidence shows that young people often tell their peers of their thoughts and plans. Of course, there are some suicides that occur without warning. But it is important to understand what the warning signs are and look out for them.

Someone who is suicidal is determined to die. The majority of people who feel suicidal do not actually want to die; they do not want to live the life they have. Often, feeling actively suicidal is temporary, even if someone has been feeling low, anxious, or struggling to cope for a long period of time. This is why getting the right kind of support at the right time is so important.

You have to be mentally ill to think about suicide. Most people have thought of suicide from time to time and not all people who die by suicide have mental health problems at the time of death. However, many people who kill themselves do suffer with their mental health, typically to a serious degree. Sometimes it's known about before the person's death and sometimes not. Approximately two thirds of people who die by suicide have not been in contact with mental health services.

Worried about self-harm?

The urge to self-harm is like a wave

It feels the most powerful when you start wanting to do it

Learn to ride the wave with the free Calm Harm app using these activities; Comfort, **Distract**, Express Yourself, Release, Random and Breathe on the Calm Harm app

When you ride the wave, the urge will fade

CALM HARM

stem4

stemming teenage mental illness
supporting teenage mental health

Download on the App Store

GET IT ON Google Play

PAPYRUS
PREVENTION OF YOUNG SUICIDE

HOPELINEUK
Call: **0800 068 4141**
Text: **07786209697**
Email: **pat@papyrus-uk.org**

Opening hours:
10am - 10pm weekdays
2pm - 10pm weekends
2pm - 10pm bank holidays

www.papyrus-uk.org

Suicidal thoughts do not have to end in suicide

HOPELINEUK

DREAMS AND WISHES:

- Go to Japan ☐
- use a public loo ☐
- make a youtube channel ☐
- Go to disney land
- become well-known

Suzi Godson

Co-founder of MeeTwo Education.
Research psychologist and author.
Sex & Relationships columnist at
The Times newspaper.

How are smartphones influencing teenagers?
It is hard to say because although millennials were
the first online cohort in history, Generation Z
are true digital natives. They have no memory
of a world before Snap, Insta or Facebook and
smartphones are an integral part of their identity.
For GenZ, digital environments are not a virtual
reality; they are reality. Today's teenagers go to
sleep by the light of a glowing screen and wake
to a mobile alarm. Social media basically lets
teenagers live in a state of perpetual contact with
their peers.

**The average teenager spends around six
hours a day looking at screens, yet we have
very limited understanding of the long term
impact of intense digital immersion.**

Existing research shows that social media and text
messaging provide feelings of intimacy, proximity
and security, and it allows teenagers to consider
what they want to say, or edit how they want
to come across. However 'anywhere, anytime'
accessibility can also give rise to contradictory
feelings of anxiety, exclusion and obligation.

Are parents right to be concerned? When we launched MeeTwo, we were waiting for young people to blame their distress on social media. We are still waiting.

Parents have inevitable concerns about issues such as cyber-bullying and the competitive nature of social media but these are often real world, rather than purely digital problems. They also profess to be profoundly anxious about uncontrolled access to sex, yet the perils of sexting and porn are rarely counter-pointed by sensible real world advice and information. Few parents feel comfortable talking about sex with their children, and schools still swerve on sex education so it is hardly surprising that in the absence of a viable alternative, the internet has become such an important resource for young people who are searching for advice and information about issues of gender, sexuality, and relationships.

In recent years, the biggest concern about smartphones is the impact that they are having on mental health. Timewise, the escalation of anxiety and depression in young people maps pretty neatly onto the emergence of digital technology. The iphone was invented in 2007 and by 2010 mental health in young people had begun its sharp decline. This correlation has been used as evidence that technology is at the heart of the current mental health crisis, but between 2007 and 2008 there was an awful lot of other stuff going on in the world.

The global financial crisis plunged the UK into the deepest recession since the 1950s. Austerity measures led to cuts in welfare, wage freezes and increased unemployment. These constraints put huge pressure on family relationships so, for example, in 2010, the divorce rate went up for the first time in seven years. For young people, pressure on parents at home, was compounded by pressure on teachers at school. And people with mental health problems were hit hardest of all. Between 2008 and 2010, an extra 846 men and 155 women committed suicide.

When you consider the impact of massive education reform, budget cuts, the selling off of playing fields, the squeeze on sport and art, the scrapping of Educational Maintenance Allowances, and the decision to increase university tuition fees to £9,000 a year, it seems a little naive to blame declining teenage mental health on 1-2-1 chat, slime videos and bunny rabbit filters.

So is tech a force for good? There are currently two opposing schools of thought about teenagers and tech. One school promotes the educational possibilities and believe that mobile tech augments social connections, helps young people to learn and makes them responsible citizens. The other interprets adolescent connectedness through a filter of fear. They argue that mobile tech ruins concentration, leads to social isolation, makes young people more vulnerable to predators and exposes them to adult themes at an early age.

Both views highlight the potential for mobile tech to influence young people, but my view is that anyone who believes social media can affect young people in a negative way must, by extension, accept that it has the potential to influence them in a positive way too.

Although the harbingers of doom focus on the perils of porn, sexting and grooming, young people are far more likely to be damaged by the false reality presented by TV shows like Love Island where having a six pack is regarded as much more important than having an IQ.

In the teenage years self-esteem is particularly fragile because young people are searching for their own identities. Judging yourself against your peers is an important part of finding out who you are, but it is a painful process because most teenagers prefer fitting in to feeling different. In adolescence, friends have a bigger impact than family on mental health, so social isolation can have a devastating impact.

Any form of bullying is problematic but we need to be careful not to throw the baby out with the bathwater. For teenagers who feel anxious, lonely, distressed or who are coping with difficulties at home, social media is a lifeline to much needed support and this was at the heart of our decision to develop the MeeTwo app.

How does the app work? From the outside it looks like a simple Twitter style social media app but it actually integrates the latest research on

peer support and positive psychology. The app also provides an important window into the issues that are worrying young people and our data is already providing important insights into adolescent mental health, both in real time and longitudinally.

When a young person uses MeeTwo they can share their anxieties in words or images and get support from peers (other teenagers), super-peers (psychology undergraduates) and experts (psychologists). However the thing that is fundamentally different about MeeTwo is that it is 100% moderated, so nothing goes into the feed before it has been checked by a human. This eliminates bullying, abuse or grooming. and ensures that young people get safe positive support. The app is anonymous, so users pick a random three word identity that is unique to MeeTwo. This allows users to be completely honest. Short 300 character posts make it quick and easy to use and educational resources are developed in response to need. MeeTwo is also a junction box to third party specialist resources and our sophisticated safeguarding systems can pick up worrying changes in a teenager's mental state, so we can redirect them to appropriate real world support services.

Do all the young people who use the MeeTwo app getting help from experts?
No. MeeTwo primarily encourages teens to use their own experiences to help each other. It also provides young people with an opportunity to see what other young people of the same age feel anxious about and this can help to normalise worries and make young people feel less isolated. This interactive process builds resilience and

creates a scalable virtuous circle where 'helping', benefits both the 'helped', and the 'helper'. There are actually experts in the background and they will occasionally offer guidance, but our goal is to teach young people how to help themselves, by helping each other. We know that young people respond better to advice from peers than to advice from adults so, for example, when we get a question about whether it is normal never to have kissed someone by the age of 16, peers are absolutely the best people to confirm that this is indeed normal and nothing to worry about.

What issues come up most on the app?
The posts on MeeTwo consistently confirm that psychological distress is almost always an interaction between individual and environmental factors. What we see, time and again, are age old problems such as family breakdown, reconstituted families, parental mental health issues, parental alcoholism, poverty, exam stress, toxic friendships, bereavement and issues to do with sexuality and sexual relationships.

When these issues are not addressed we see an escalation in coping mechanisms such as cutting, panic attacks, depression and eating disorders as young people desperately try to find a way to control chaotic feelings.

Many of our young users come from difficult home environments, but many more are bottling up feelings because they don't want to worry their parents, or let them down. Sometimes their parents are too preoccupied with issues of their own to notice what is going on. At other times, it is the weight of parental expectation that is pushing kids to breaking point.

Academic pressure compounds the problem. Continuous testing starts as soon as kids return after the holidays and although most of these tests are simply to allow a teacher to judge whether a child is making progress, for a young person, every test is an opportunity to fail, to be criticised and to feel less adequate than other people in their class.

Can an app really make a difference? There is no magic wand for mental health issues, but for teenagers who feel anxious, confused and alone, the MeeTwo app now means that they can have free, safe, immediate personal support and advice in their pocket. We know that early intervention can stop mental health issues escalating to crisis point but the threshold for access to Child and Adolescent Mental Health Services (CAMHS) is now so high that only the most severe cases get treated. This means that low cost, innovative and scalable solutions like MeeTwo are becoming increasingly important. We are now working with the NHS to find ways to use what we are learning about young people and the issues they are struggling with to inform and improve care.

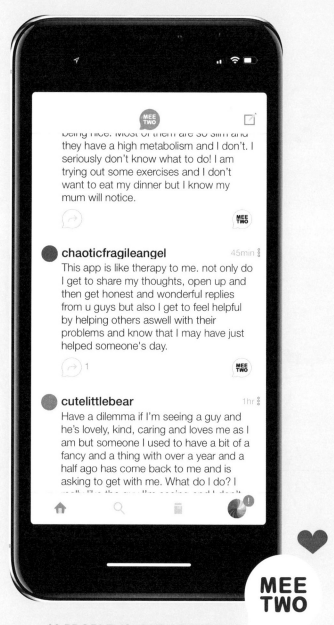

being nice. Most of them are so slim and they have a high metabolism and I don't. I seriously don't know what to do! I am trying out some exercises and I don't want to eat my dinner but I know my mum will notice.

chaoticfragileangel   45min

This app is like therapy to me. not only do I get to share my thoughts, open up and then get honest and wonderful replies from u guys but also I get to feel helpful by helping others aswell with their problems and know that I may have just helped someone's day.

cutelittlebear   1hr

Have a dilemma if I'm seeing a guy and he's lovely, kind, caring and loves me as I am but someone I used to have a bit of a fancy and a thing with over a year and a half ago has come back to me and is asking to get with me. What do I do? I

MEE TWO

99 PROBLEMS. ONE SOLUTION

LESSON ✳ 6

HAVE CAKE AND TEA WITH YOUR DEMONS

Yumi Sakugawa

To all the girls in the younger years,
I spent a lot of time thinking about what prank I should do for yr13 leavers day.
When I thought about it almost everything I could think of had been done. So
instead I decided to do something a little more worthwhile and write this lame
note.
When I was in yr7-9 I had very low self esteem; I hated the way I looked, my
personality, I even doubted my intelligence. You may laugh at this note but I
wanted you all to know that you are loved, even if you don't think you are.
I wanted to say the best life lesson you'll ever learn is to respect yourself, and
that the love of your life will be you. You have to spend the rest of your life
with yourself so be kind to her! Do not hurt or criticise yourself, nurture
yourself and make sure to be kind to yourself during your years here. Be kind
to the girls around you because we are all too tough on ourselves growing up.
Do not tear eachother down, show one another the same kindness you need.

- A girl from yr13

Henrietta Bowden-Jones

Consultant psychiatrist
specialisng in addictions.
Vice President of
The Medical Women's Federation

Why do you think so many young people are struggling with anxiety and depression?
I believe that the immediacy of today's society, in terms of consumerism, and the availability of things, whether it is getting a takeaway, or buying a book, is problematic, because people are used to an immediacy in terms of rewards and it adds an urgency to people's responses. However, young people are now communicating their distress via social media and the internet in a way previous generations were unable to do. Some of that sharing helps them cope more with difficult feelings and the information they receive from their online searches can make people recognise they may need help for mental health symptoms.

I think there's been a speeding up of emotional processes and that's partly why there is so much 'catastrophising'. It comes from not taking time to examine the different components of feelings and events. It means that things are never just bad, they are very, very bad, and then it's suicidal thinking, it's self-harm, its "this is the end" and there's no point in carrying on.

Some of the intensity of these feelings begins to decrease in one's early 20s and we see a spontaneous remission in many of the more impulsive presentations. Of course people with significant mental health problems will continue to have them and age does not cure it at all! Whether it is pathological gambling, gaming, sex addiction, or just people with depression and anxiety, they get to an age in their mid 20s where they are more objective about their feelings and are more able to postpone gratification or just be more measured about the intensity of their responses. Of course, if we're talking about severe and enduring mental illness, someone with severe depression and suicidality will wake up tomorrow, and they'll still be feeling the same or worse, so we are making a distinction between someone with a mental illness and someone who is feeling intense negative thoughts as part of a normal life.

Is technology the problem? There are pros and cons to technology as we know, but for people like me who work with technological addiction, its pervasive influence on so many platforms. Social media can present as a problem to some people because every time they post something, if people like it, you get a sense of pleasure. It is not an intense pleasure, but I would say that by the time you're getting hundreds of likes on a post, or retweets, that can be confusing to some and lead people to closely link feelings of self confidence and identity to how much recognition they get online. If as a young person you start to over rely on other people's opinions, or measure your achievements in terms of numbers of followers, then it is time to put the tech away for a bit and focus on real life friendships and schoolwork!

Children are less able to postpone gratification. This skill develops with age and because their frontal lobes are not fully mature, they are less likely to exert moderation, and this is at the core of being able to not do something you enjoy because you know you've done too much of it already. Sensation seeking is also heightened in the young and this carries risks online so there is a need for good blocking software for porn and gambling sites.

How do you know when a young person is using technology in a harmful way? It's about the consequences. I have had patients who were in school or university but they were still putting in eight hours of gaming a day. These people often do gaming and porn together, because it is hard to do porn for eight hours and it's hard to do gaming for eight hours, so they split the time in between, with a bit of telly added in as a cocktail. I don't see it so much in girls, but the boys have a really clear pattern of TV, porn and gaming and they gradually remove themselves more and more, and isolate and become very taciturn and they will not share. The more they don't share, the more they accumulate distress.

Once the isolation is so extreme, schools and parents are concerned and urge them to get help. Their big fear, of course, is that one morning they will go upstairs and their child will be dead because there was something terrible going on that they didn't know about such as blackmailing, or extreme bullying or severe debts from gambling.

Is the number of hours spent gaming a key indicator? The number of hours is one of the ways loss of control is identified. Problem gamers get to an extreme stage of not leaving their room, they eat in their bed, they live on cereal and they do that for weeks and weeks on end until someone intervenes, or they seek help.

When young people are gaming obsessively and in a pathological way they stop performing academically. It is so sad to see people with great aspirations, who used to be the high achievers in the family, gradually under perform to a point of not fulfilling any of the expected grades, or indeed dropping out of school or university completely.

Having to repeat the year comes with big issues in terms of fitting in with one's peer group and people report the fear of feeling stupid because they haven't achieved their original goals. So many young patients we have seen have not returned to university for fear of being judged.

What about porn? Excessive use of porn is another problem. Aside from the sheer number of hours people can spend online watching porn, it is also the unsafe encounters it can lead to. We know that people can put themselves at risk on webcams doing all sorts of things and having encounters with grown-ups without their parents knowing. Although people are normally older, sometimes they start at 14 or 15, at times with significant peer pressure.

A lot of them are vulnerable young boys who are not interpersonally skilled, so they're often quite isolated at school too. They are struggling, they might be reserved, they might be bullied. Sometimes there are sexuality issues and I have met young patients who were leading an onlife life that differed from their real life relationships.

They don't know where they fit, or whether their sexuality fits comfortably with them, or their families, or their peers, so they go online to find out more. They might originally go online to find out more in a kind of academic way, but the availability of all sorts of material distracts them, and sometimes they end up watching a lot of porn. There have been some patients who think they are heterosexual but are watching five hours of homosexual porn online, and this is very confusing so then they think, well maybe I'll go to a chat room.

When they end up in chat rooms, that's when things get complicated because the power of older, more predatory people, over a young vulnerable unclear mind, is enormous. And that's when they get on to webcams. And then there is guilt and shame and blackmail and it is impossible to share with their parents, so they're desperate to sort it out. They are frightened because it could come out. They regret it but it's out there.

Presumably it is just as difficult for gambling addicts to tell their parents? Young gamblers are sometimes online with their parents' credit cards and you only meet them when the parents march them in because the parents were on holiday and when they came back all their money was gone. You know it's not an uncommon scenario. The lucky ones are the ones who are able to acknowledge that there is a problem and tell teachers, or whoever it may be, that there is a problem, or the ones who get caught.

The other big issue for young people is that an early big win is a majorly destructive force. It somehow disregulates their perception of reward and makes them take on somehow an erroneous cognitive construct that makes them feel that if they play the machine, they will be receiving the same amount of money and if they don't, they just continue to try. They end up chasing losses, which is a classic symptom in problem gamblers.

This also happens when young people witness a close friend having a big win. It means that a whole group of people can be catastrophically affected by one big win which is why I campaign very hard to keep young people away from any sort of gambling at all.

Can you predict whether a child will have addictive tendencies? Karen Ersche's research shows that impulsivity at the age of seven is the greatest predictor for who is at risk of problem gambling in later life. That is fascinating to me, because it shows that there is a lot of

preventative work that we can do. There are often complexities to the family environments and to the backgrounds so a more systemic approach to supporting the whole family can help. When helping with gaming disorder, we really need to re-educate the family about eating meals together, to encourage healthy activities and sport. Structure is vital. By the time I see people with these behavioural addictions they've lost all structure and to regain a sense of structure even if it's imposed from above, gives them a sense of hope, when all hope has gone.

The young people in my clinic talk about being in utter chaos internally and externally because often, their behaviour has caused ripples in the family and there is discordance in the families. Children who understand the repercussions of their problematic behaviour feel guilty and anxious and this triggers more problematic behaviour.

How are behavioural addictions treated?
A cognitive behavioural approach has been shown to work well. It centres around eight sessions that identify triggers and plan ways to neutralise them. Stimulus control to reduce or prevent compulsive behaviours is a major component. Software is installed so that people are not able to access porn or gambling websites.

Stopping people from carrying money or cards also plays a part, so a mother will make her son a sandwich, rather than giving him money to buy

lunch, because she knows that he will spend it on gambling and he won't eat. You need to break the cycle and once you do that, it becomes easier to resist the urge. Eventually that automatic constant loop disintegrates and it can be replaced by more positive behavioural drives like sport. I try to get all my patients to exercise. Recording the activity, and making time for it in their diaries every day, five times a week, becomes as important as the rest of the treatment really.

A lot of people with the tendency to go to extremes turn to ultra-running because their dopaminergic rewards systems actually needs a higher intensity of stimulus to be able to give them the same pleasure. Doing a 10k is not enough for them!

What percentage of addiction is genetic? Genetics plays a big part in addiction, including behavioural ones. Problem gamblers at our clinic often have parents or grandparents who gambled. However, environment is also important, as early life negative events such as abandonment, trauma and abuse all can lead a person to take refuge into addictive behaviours.

Before founding the National Problem Gambling Clinic in 2008, I ran the detox centre for the NHS for drugs and alcohol in central London. At the time there was less Internet availability as people did not often have smartphones and so those young people seen were pretty much prisoners of their environments. When the parents were abusive they ran away from home very young and ended up being subjected to very unpleasant stuff and getting into drugs.

Nowadays, we've got a situation where a lot of the people I see are still living in very unpleasant situations, but technology helps them because they can get support so there are significant positives about being connected and having the ability to seek help this way.

For those young people, technology helps to remove them from the incarceration of a very, very bad family life. Being able to access help and information is vital because young people in difficult situations will often seek help from websites where other young people are sharing similar problems.

Does tech make it harder to forget bad experiences? Yes. There's a whole issue about your online history and how you've got the right to forget, the right to move on. It must be extremely difficult for people who have been through episodes of low self esteem, self harm, self disgust, to then have that memory and that existence in the eyes of others. Because even when you delete things, others may have kept things in order to have power over you, so some of the young people that come to see me have very complex digital histories that are causing them stress.

Before digital times, difficult things you did or said, became forgotten or cloudy as you got older, including extremely difficult things that one had lived, because memory also serves a purifying function at some level.

What can parents do to help? I really, really, really believe that we should limit exposure to digital platforms in terms of number of hours when children are growing up. Young brains need some down time. They need to read, to be creative, to exercise. You need to create mental space in order to start anything positive and some people are now moving away from smartphones for this very reason, particularly our patients who do not wish to relapse. They are using old fashioned phones instead, because otherwise they can't resist the urge.

The ultimate goal is to get people to turn their phones off at home and school, or to remove them from their proximity because these young people's phone are literally constantly buzzing so it's impacting on their concentration and focus.

Do you think we need internet regulation? Definitely. I think that there is an enormous amount of work to be done by the gaming industry in particular. The gambling industry is going through it at the moment. Gaming has not even started. Virtual reality has not even been touched.

There are major pieces of legislation that need to happen, but I think it will come down to people deciding that there is more pleasure in other activities and by setting this example, they will begin to lead their peers.

I think that we are already seeing that in terms of exercise. A lot of young people are choosing to go to the gym and choosing to get fit instead of being on their phones, because they themselves realise it is impacting them in terms of obesity levels, in terms of focus, in terms of happiness.

We have been through a war in relation to technology, but we could be coming through to the other side.

Ruby Evans I ♥ her
Germany 1918 - 1939
History
Miss Gall-Gray

History History History

Weimar
Germany
♪: Germany.

Beggin'
oon-oon-oon

Sir Anthony Seldon

Vice-Chancellor,
The University of Buckingham.
Political historian and educationalist

What can we do to improve mental health in young people? The way to improve mental health is to help young people to recognize that they are moral agents who are responsible for their own levels of happiness or unhappiness. I think we infantilise our young people and we make them into victims by making them feel that they have no efficacy. If you blame conditions, blame other people for your unhappiness, the unhappiness will continue.

Learned helplessness describes how people stop trying to change if they believe that they can't do something. It is the common characteristic of the depressive, the highly anxious, the eating disordered, the angry person, the lost person. These people have learned to be helpless and in order to change that, they have to learn efficacy and how to be responsible for themselves.

I think the whole approach of the NHS is built around helplessness and the all-powerful state. Saying "Don't worry, we'll look after you" is unhelpful actually. What is helpful is to say "Don't worry, we'll help you look after yourself" but that doesn't suit the NHS institutionally, or philosophically, which is why illness in this country is growing, rather than decreasing.

What we should be doing is teaching our young people how to avoid being physically and mentally ill. If we use the analogy of a waterfall, what we do at the moment is, we wait for people to hit the bottom of the waterfall and then we rush in and say "this is terrible". Once somebody has hit the bottom, it's much harder to put them back together again, and it costs a lot more money. We should be working at the top of the waterfall instead.

We need to accept that the current of life will always lead some young people towards the edge of the waterfall, so we need to give all of them the skills to stop themselves going over the edge. We need to teach them how to cope for themselves, to develop character and resilience, so that they are able to resist those currents and manage their lives in a way that stops them getting to crisis point.

Unfortunately, our current model of health-care is institutionalised and paternalistic, not individualistic. It is designed to provide patronising help in the best possible way, often with medication, and it doesn't help people to help themselves.

It is better to give somebody a rod than to give them a fish. It respects the human spirit and maintains a person's dignity. And it is natural. We are flinging chemicals into people at the moment. We have a war on lethal drugs. We should be having a war on legal drugs too. In the short term they may be helpful, but in the long term, they are not doing anything.

Do you think mental health issues in young people are being compounded by the education system? In my book 'An End To Factory Schools' I explain that we've had three educational revolutions. The first, five million years ago, was the beginning of learning. Then, five thousand years ago, we had the beginning of organised learning, and five hundred years ago, we had the beginning of mass education with the factory model.

The factory model is only interested in mass, measurable, quantifiable results. It doesn't treat children as individuals. It treats them as passive receptors into which deposits of knowledge are made. And children are validated by their ability to reproduce the right information, at the right time, in the right way. This does not individuate people, it homogenises them.

Too many young people feel that they are not worthwhile because the education system is not interested in them, and doesn't value them. People don't feel valuable when they are judged on their grades, rather than their abilities, or their passions. It's actually cruel. I think it's a form of abuse of young people, and it will be seen to be so in the future. It's not the fault of the teachers, it's the fault of the system. We are locked into this way of thinking and it is contributing very significantly to mental illness in young people.

Before the first world war they developed intelligence tests which all exams are still modelled on, but when they looked at the results of these

tests they found something totally extraordinary. They found that the people who did best in the intelligence tests were just like the people who devised the tests at the University. They were male. They were white. They were middle class. They were cognitive thinkers. This is belittling to human beings because it narrows down what it is to be human and means that people who don't conform to a constructed set of measures automatically fail.

One of the most important people and least well known in all of this field is Howard Gardner at Harvard. He said "don't ask how intelligent a child is, ask rather, how is a child intelligent?" If you want to know how intelligent a child is, a university IQ test will give you a very precise, but very limited measure. When you ask how 'is' a child intelligent you understand that all children are intelligent in different ways.

How should we be teaching children? We had a teacher's conference two weeks ago at the Royal Shakespeare Company and one of the teachers who was there said that a child had read out a story in his class about somebody who wasn't loved, and one of the other children had stood up and said "I don't feel loved by my parents. I don't think my parents love me". This is the beginning of the kind of learning that we need in schools, but it is suppressed, not because the people in the DfE and Ofsted are evil bad people, but because they are locked into a mindset which is so all pervasive that they can't even see that it's happening. The irony of course is that when I was

head of Wellington College, we put happiness first and we went up on The Sunday Times league table for A level results from 256th to 21st in the whole country. No school had ever done that before and yet at the same time, we were leading on wellbeing too.

So if wellbeing comes first everything else follows? Yes, but there is good and bad wellbeing. Bad wellbeing is done in an infantilising way that stops people really being pressed academically. Challenge is a good thing.

There's a lobby in the wellbeing industry that sees pressure on people as bad. That's rubbish. Pressure is good and stress is inevitable, so you need to be able to cope with it. Stress makes our lives worthwhile.

We need a lot more stress in life. We need to get our young people going on long walks, going on adventures, going rock climbing, doing things where they are testing themselves and being put in stressful situations. To succeed is the reward and that's how young people grow. And, actually the results go up too, so parents are doubly happy.

How do we encourage mental resilience and wellbeing in young people? First, is to recognise that you are responsible. If anyone's ever told you to blame others, don't believe it. You can materially affect your own level of happiness, so if you want to reduce the times that you feel tight and anxious and angry and disconnected and low and sullen and alienated and lonely, there are things that you can do to change those feelings.

More than anything else in the Universe, relationships have the power to make us happy or unhappy, but the golden rule of relationships is to treat others in the way that we would like to be treated ourselves.

Ultimately, if we see other people as ourselves, we feel better about life. Brothers, sisters, parents, aunts, uncles, grandparents, teachers, mates at school, what we put into those relationships is what we get out. It is also important to recognise that our physical bodies are systems that we need to treat well. We lavish love on our possessions, but we don't often think about our bodies. Our bodies are quite basic systems. They need to be watered and nourished with food that is natural and unprocessed. We need to rest, to sleep, to let our minds turn off and we need to exercise to keep the body strong. If we don't take care of our physical body we feel lethargic and we don't feel proud of it either, which can make us feel anxious and depressed. If we look after the body, we feel good.

You are a big advocate for mindfulness, but how easy is it for a young person to learn from an app? Well, I've spent 40 years doing mindfulness and I'm still really bad at it. I wish I was better. I keep forgetting and my mind keeps going off, so it's a very difficult process. Young people don't have to learn to meditate but it is very important to help them recognise that anxious thoughts are mental events and that they will pass. I think we should be trying to build that capacity into all young people, which is why I would like all schools to spend time in each day when the

children are in silence, where they learn just to be still with themselves. It's a great insight that comes from Quaker schools. I often used stillness and calming exercises at Wellington, particularly before the exams. If the mind is calm but alert, students are more likely to read the questions correctly and do their best. It helps bring us to a position of self-acceptance where the all-conquering mind is pacified.

With regard to apps, I think young people use whatever the language of the time is, and apps are one of the forms of communications that they're used to, but mindfulness is a lifelong project and I'm quite sceptical about some of the claims about benefits that are made by mindfulness apps. By itself, at best, mindfulness may help people to live with themselves without resorting to a gin and tonic, or a spliff, or unloving relationships, but that's it. These apps also seem to make a lot of money out of it and that doesn't sit well with me.

One of the key messages I try to get across is that the accumulation of excessive money, or power, or status, is both unhealthy and unhelpful. I want the world to be a space where people genuinely understand the difference between pleasure and happiness. Pleasure is what we get when we treat other people and objects, as something that exists to please us. Happiness is what we get when we show care and compassion to others.

MEE
TWO

Directory